ADVOCACY IN THE MAGISTRATES' COURT

Cavendish
Publishing
Limited

London • Sydney • Portland, Oregon

ADVOCACY IN THE MAGISTRATES' COURT

James Welsh, BA, Dip Law
Certified Inns Advocacy Trainer
Head of Advocacy Training, BPP Law School
Practising Door Tenant, Bedford Row

Cavendish
Publishing
Limited

London • Sydney • Portland, Oregon

First published in Great Britain 2003 by
Cavendish Publishing Limited, The Glass House,
Wharton Street, London WC1X 9PX, United Kingdom
Telephone: + 44 (0)20 7278 8000   Facsimile: + 44 (0)20 7278 8080
Email: info@cavendishpublishing.com
Website: www.cavendishpublishing.com

Published in the United States by Cavendish Publishing
c/o International Specialized Book Services,
5824 NE Hassalo Street, Portland,
Oregon 97213-3644, USA

Published in Australia by Cavendish Publishing (Australia) Pty Ltd
45 Beach Street, Coogee, NSW 2034, Australia
Telephone: + 61 (2)9664 0909   Facsimile: + 61 (2)9664 5420
Email: info@cavendishpublishing.com.au
Website: www.cavendishpublishing.com.au

© Welsh, James   2003

British Library Cataloguing in Publication Data
Welsh, James
Advocacy in the magistrates' court
1 Criminal procedure – England 2 Criminal procedure – Wales
I Title
345.4'2'05

Library of Congress Cataloguing in Publication Data
Data available

ISBN 1-85941-784-1

3 5 7 9 10 8 6 4

Printed and bound by CPI Antony Rowe, Eastbourne

Acknowledgments

For the inside guidance on how to successfully apply for public funding, and for being a superb court clerk, I would like to thank:

> Roy Alec Campbell – BSc, LLB, Solicitor, Legal Adviser, Plymouth District Magistrates Court.

For their help on the chapters on youth courts and road traffic, I am most grateful to:

> Keeley Harvey (1999 call) – 18 Carlton Crescent, Southampton.

> Rachel Goodall (2000 call) – 18 Carlton Crescent, Southampton.

And for a host of good ideas, I would like to thank:

> Abigail Webb (2001 call).

Contents

Contents

xi

Introduction

What is the purpose of this book?

This book is not a textbook. It will not attempt to teach you the law. This book is designed to give you a practical and realistic guide as to what to do when you are appearing in the magistrates' court with little or no prior experience. Some parts of this book have been reproduced from the first edition of *Criminal Advocacy* (also published by Cavendish Publishing).

The book attempts to be distinctive in taking a direct and practical approach in telling the advocate where to go and who to speak to. It is the sort of advice that practitioners can be embarrassed to ask their colleagues. It is also the kind of advice that can help prevent having the court, your client or the clerks yelling at you!

I have tried to keep the language simple and direct. I have tried to imagine that you have been sent to court with potentially very little notice and you want an overview of the procedure and the sorts of issues that commonly occur in hearings like the one that you have been sent to. I have produced summaries and checklists where I think that they may assist you.

I have endeavoured to use the *real* language that you will hear at court, and I have tried to pass on some tips that are very practical and 'real' and which are not covered in other texts. The advice on filling in a 'Form A' for public funding is an example of the sort of practical assistance that this book hopes to share with you.

Who is the book aimed at?

The author is a barrister, and the author's natural sympathies are with pupil barristers starting their second six months of pupillage. The book should be equally relevant to defence solicitors who are appearing in court in the early days of their practice. There are not many references to keep the clerks happy and they are easily ignored if you are a solicitor!

How about prosecutors?

This book is aimed primarily at defence lawyers and most of the commentary is directed to the task of defending. Many pupils will be asked to prosecute and so where there are any very important and clear words of advice for those holding the files for the Crown Prosecution Service these have been included. The summaries of procedure include when the prosecutor will speak and what they might address, and so to that end the book will help both parties.

Terminology

The book seeks to help the advocate with all the jargon that might be encountered at the magistrates' court. There is a glossary of jargon in the book. Where the area of proceedings is particularly beset with problems of terminology, these are dealt with in the particular chapters.

Advice on conferencing/interviewing is also included

Few books make any attempt to help advocates with what might be wise or unwise to say to a client in conference. There are some pitfalls to be avoided in conducting conferences, and there are some pointers to help the advocate's credibility. Where these arise, they are included in the book. For example, there is some advice on when it might be useful to talk about remand privileges before considering whether to make a bail application or to plead guilty.

The structure

The basic structure is to look at each stage in the proceedings in turn. Therefore, if you know that you are going to perform a 'first appearance' you can simply turn to the 'first appearance' section and take it from there.

Glossary

AI/AD	Advance information/disclosure.
ABH	Assault occasioning actual bodily harm contrary to s 47 of the Offences Against the Person Act 1861.
CAD	Computer Aided Dispatch Transcript of communication between a police vehicle and the police station (eg, commentary on a pursuit).
Form/previous	Previous convictions.
FTA/FTS	Failure to attend court/failure to surrender to court.
Go up	Eg, 'This case is going up' meaning that the case will be committed to the Crown Court.
IRB	Incident report book. Police officer's notebook in which the officer will write up the events of a case as soon as it is practicable to do so.
Indictable	Any case that could be heard in the Crown Court (on an indictment).
Half time	The point in the trial after the close of the prosecution case but before the start of the defence case.
HORT/1 (often pronounced 'horti')	This is the demand from the police to a driver to produce the vehicle's and driver's documents (licence, insurance, etc).
MG 11	Witness statement form.
Neary court	A court hearing first appearances.
NFA	No further action.
Old style committal	A committal with a consideration of the evidence.

OIC	The officer in the case. It is the OIC who is primarily responsible for the handling of the case from the police end. The OIC is the one to ask about exhibits, the investigation, the interview, etc.
PDH	A plea and directions hearing. This is the hearing at the Crown Court for cases committed to the Crown Court by the magistrates' court.
Plead	As in plead guilty.
PTR	Pre-trial review.
Previous	*See* Form.
Section 9 statement	A statement that has been agreed by both parties, so that the evidence contained therein can be read out rather than having to call the witness.
Section 47	Section 47 of the Offences Against the Person Act 1861 is the offence of actual bodily harm. This section is so common it is usually simply referred to by the section number, or as ABH. *See* ABH.
SOCO	Scene of the crimes officer. The SOCO will be in charge of matters like taking fingerprints and other forensic evidence.
Stay down	Remain in the magistrates' court.
TDA	Taking and driving away.
TWOC	Taking a vehicle without consent. Often used as a verb: 'He was caught twoc-ing'.
TIC	Offences taken into consideration when sentencing.

Video court/ video link court	Some courts can now 'hook up' to their local prisons, and conferences and court appearances can be dealt with on video link. See Chapter 19 for more information.
VO	A 'visiting order', ie, what the prison service gives out so that a prisoner can have a visitor. Client may say, 'Tell Cheryl I'll send her a VO'.

1   Getting to court

It's time to go to court. If you want to be at the right court at the right time, it's worth doing your homework on how to get there first!

Check the destination

Don't assume that the court to which you have been told to go is the correct one. Check the papers and look at previous endorsements on the brief or a notice from the court. In particular, check for the following:

- Transfers from one local court to another to make listing easier, eg, from Ealing to Acton.

- Where a defendant has matters outstanding in another court, the case may have been transferred to that court so that all matters can be dealt with together.

- Some courts sit at a number of different places, especially youth courts which can sit at one place on one day and another on a different day.

- Be careful with courts with similar names, eg, Brentford, Brentwood and Brent.

If the location or time of the hearing is unclear, ring the court and ask for the listing office. Be ready to quote the case name and number.

An invaluable guide to courts on the south-eastern and western Circuits is *The Court Guide* by Andrew Goodman (2001, London: Blackstone). It gives the address, telephone number, opening times and facilities and directions for travel by public or private transport for all the courts on those two Circuits. However, the guide is not annual and the details are not always up to date. The directions are not detailed and it is well worth leaving a little extra time if you are going somewhere for the first time. For other courts, see *Shaw's Directory of Courts* (2003, London: Shaw & Sons Ltd), which is published annually, although this does not give directions.

What to take with you

It really does not matter what you take to write on, but it is important to start keeping records of all cases that you have done. A client could choose to make a complaint a year after the case is concluded, and advocates must be able to find their record of what took place. Most barristers favour taking the blue 'counsel's notebooks'. It is a good idea to write on the cover the name and date of all cases for which you used that notebook and then store the notebooks chronologically for several years. Files with loose-leaf paper are quite bulky and may prove awkward to carry around at court and they will certainly be more problematic to store.

Apart from the obvious (paper, pens, etc) it would be unwise to go to court without a reliable text on the law. Many junior practitioners prefer *Blackstone's Criminal Practice (Blackstone's)* (2003, Oxford: OUP) to *Archbold: Pleading, Evidence and Practice (Archbold)* (2002, London: Sweet & Maxwell) for use in the magistrates' court. In many ways, *Blackstone's* is an easier text to use and it covers more magistrates' court procedure. *Archbold* is a more informative text for the Crown Court. Antony and Berryman's *Magistrates' Court Guide* (2002, London: Butterworths) is another useful book covering most offences routinely dealt with in the magistrates' court but it is in practice only acceptable to quote *Archbold* or *Blackstone's* in court.

From time to time advocates find that they need tissues for crying clients.

Take a mobile phone to court if you have one. It may be that the advocate needs to telephone the client to see where he is if he has not attended on time. Barrister's clerks like to be able to keep in contact with their barristers so that if any work arrives in chambers for the court at which you may be appearing, the clerks can offer to cover the work. It is bad practice for a phone to go off in conference and it is unprofessional if it rings in court. The best practice is to turn the phone off on arrival at court but to check for messages whenever there is a chance.

How to dress

The standard of dress in the magistrates' court is varied and it is extremely rare for a magistrate to comment on an advocate's dress. However, this should not act as a licence to dress inappropriately and it is best to err on the side of caution. Suits should be dark and sober, and shirts should not be too bright or garish. Avoid ties that depict cartoons or are otherwise frivolous. Criminal clients may well judge their advocate on appearances. Defendants should not feel that their advocate is less smart or formal than the other advocates that they see at court.

Prosecutors

Courts can accommodate defence advocates being late far more readily than they can accommodate having no prosecutor. If you have an unavoidable problem and you are seriously held up, then there is little that can be done but for everyone to wait and make the best job of catching up when you arrive. In these circumstances, call the court and let them know.

Most Crown Prosecution Service (CPS) offices cannot send out papers in advance, and so the papers will be at court, and other prosecutors may be able to cover your work for you.

What if ...?

• *You oversleep, get held up or are sent to court late?*

Telephone the court and explain what has happened, giving the name of the case and saying how long you think you will be. Failing that, telephone your clerk or office and ask them to notify the court. Unless you are attending for a trial, the case is likely to be listed in a long list of other cases and the magistrates or judge will have plenty of other matters to deal with while you are on your way. In very busy courts, you may not even be missed!

If you are sent to court at the last minute, it is likely that the client was arrested overnight, and will be 'produced' in custody. If this is the case, the chances are that the client will be even later than you. There are notorious problems with getting prisoners distributed to the various magistrates' courts, and sometimes defence lawyers have to wait until about midday before the van of prisoners arrives.

If you are listed for a trial or other matter where the court has set aside time for a long hearing, what will happen will depend on how late you are. It may still be possible to hear the case, or it may have to be adjourned to another day. If it seems that you will be unable to reach court until fairly late in the day, maintain contact with the court as you may be told that there is no point in your attending court at all.

Whenever you arrive late, apologise to the client and to the court if it has been kept waiting. You may arrive too late to speak to the prosecutor as the proceedings are already in session. If a lay bench is sitting, there will be times when the magistrates will rise to make decisions. Look out for one of these moments and speak to the prosecutor during this period. If a District Judge is sitting, there may be no break in the proceedings. Sit in court for a while and wait for a good moment to approach the prosecutor.

For gathering information generally, see Chapter 2.

- *You are caught between two courts?*

In busy chambers, or at a busy firm, you may have been asked to cover one court in the morning and a different court in the afternoon. If your morning work looks as though it might overrun into the afternoon, you will need to make provision to have your afternoon work covered.

If you are a barrister, contact the clerks as soon as you foresee a problem arising. Do not contact the solicitors unless or until you have spoken to the clerks first. The clerks will have the diaries of the other members of chambers who may be available to take over the afternoon work for you. It may be better to have someone come and take over the case that was originally listed in the morning and leave you to appear in the case listed in the other court in the afternoon. Much will depend on the complexity of the cases and which case can be covered most expeditiously.

Make sure that the court knows of your difficulty; the court might take your case earlier than they otherwise would if it means that you would then be available for afternoon work.

2   On arrival

Note: if you are arriving at court with no information at all, see 'The post-it note brief', below.

Step 1: find the case name on the list

This is the first thing to do, just in case you are at the wrong court and need to set off to somewhere else immediately. The court list is usually posted up somewhere near the court entrance or it may be held by a security guard at the door or by a court usher. Ask someone to point you in the right direction. If your client's name is not on the list, go to the 'What if ...?' section of this chapter.

Step 2: make your way to the advocates' room

Most magistrates' courts have an advocates' room. You may need to find out from the usher or security guard the security code to get in or ask them to unlock the door for you. Leave your coat and briefcase in the room. It is poor etiquette to walk into court with bags and briefcases. Discreet handbags are fine for women, otherwise it is best to only bring the case papers into court.

Step 3: introduce yourself to your client

Defendants on bail will usually be bailed to attend court 30 minutes before the hearing time. Try to introduce yourself to them soon after they arrive so that they know you are there to represent them. You will often find yourself in a very busy court area full of lawyers, witnesses and defendants with no idea of what your client looks like. Call out the defendant's name. In a large court there may be a public-address system and you can ask for a call to go out. If the usher has arrived, ask if the defendant has booked in.

If the defendant is in custody, consider speaking to the prosecutor first and collecting any papers before you go to the cells. Gaining access to the cells is often time-consuming due to security so you will want to limit the number of trips you make.

Step 4: speak to the prosecutor

In the magistrates' court defence advocates may need to speak to the Crown Prosecution Service (CPS) representative or whoever is prosecuting to check what will be happening at the hearing. Once the court session has begun, it is difficult to speak to the prosecutor who will be busy dealing with other cases, so it is best to find them as early as possible. Go to the CPS room and ask who is prosecuting in the court number where your case is listed. You may have to queue behind other advocates or you may be told to come back later as the prosecutor has to sort out the files first. Make sure you are polite as there is no point in annoying the CPS representative. Shortly before the court session begins, the prosecutors will make their way into court and it may be easier to make contact there.

There are various reasons for seeing the prosecutor, eg, to obtain advance information (see Chapter 5), to plea bargain (see Chapter 10), to find out what objections there may be to bail (see Chapter 6), or to ask if the Prosecution will seek summary trial or committal (see Chapter 9).

Step 5: sign in with the usher

In many courts the ushers do not appear until 10 or 15 minutes before the session is due to start. Let the usher know that you have arrived. Your name will be written down and you may be given a slip to complete. If you think you will need more time or have received a message that your client will be arriving late, warn the usher and ask for other matters in the list to be called on first. However, if the case is going to be very short, you might persuade the usher to call the case more quickly. The case may be listed in a very long remand list and the usher will have the difficult task of juggling the order of cases. Bear this in mind when you speak to the usher: smile and be polite!

The post-it note brief

It is not uncommon to be asked to go to court with no information other than the defendant's name. If you are counsel, typically a clerk will hand you a post-it note with only a name on it.

What you want to avoid is starting a conference with:

Hello, I'm representing you, what are you charged with?

Clients want to feel that their advocates are aware of the facts of their case, and so you should avoid starting a conference without even knowing what the charge is. What follows is a digest of who knows what, and how to get information.

- *The usher/list caller*

Most courts combine these two roles. The court has a list of cases for the day, which has on it the defendant's name, a number for the court's use and a list of the charges. The usher/list caller will have this list and should be able to tell you what your client is charged with. The usher/list caller will normally only appear 10 or 15 minutes or so before the list is due to start (usually 10 am). If you explain that you have had no prior instructions, you will normally find them sympathetic, and they will not seek to call your case too soon.

- *The prosecutor*

There is a CPS office in almost all courts, and that is a good place to start when trying to find your prosecutor. You may find that your prosecutor is ready and waiting to brief you, and even to give you some disclosure.

The prosecutors are under pressure, having large numbers of files and little preparation time. In London, it is more likely than not that the prosecutor will have the files sent to court on the morning of the hearing. As a consequence, some prosecutors do not want to spend valuable time discussing the cases with defence lawyers. Therefore, it can be hard to get their attention to answer any queries you may have.

Some prosecutors will shut themselves away until just before the list starts, and it is hard to catch them before the court is called to session. If there is a lay bench, you only need to wait for the bench to rise to consider a decision, and then you can approach the prosecutor and find out something about the case. You may have more of a problem if a District Judge is sitting since the proceedings are likely to be conducted at pace. The best that you can do is to pass a note to the prosecutor who will try to answer you when they have a spare moment.

Getting time to speak to the prosecutor is an occupational difficulty of defending in the magistrates' court.

How to conduct a conference when you have almost no instructions

The simple but important trick is to conceal your lack of information. The focus of any question is that you are adding to your knowledge. It is better to appear to be asking for clarification, and hearing the defendant's version of events, even if, in reality, it is the only version that you have. For example:

> Now I know that you are charged with criminal damage. What will help me is to hear you describe the events in your own words.

It is not your fault if there has been no disclosure yet in the case, so remain proactive, for example:

> I will be working hard to get some information from the Prosecution, but in the meantime, you tell me all that you can about the arrest and what happened leading up to it.

Prosecutors

When the CPS books agents to prosecute on their behalf, the booking is normally for either a half-day or a full day. There could be almost any number of files to deal with in a day and it is rare for the CPS to send over the files in advance. If there is a single case running as a trial then there is a reasonable chance that the papers will be made available the day before.

Otherwise, the papers are sent over by courier and tend to arrive at court at around 9 am.

This can mean that prosecutors have to prepare considerable numbers of cases in a short space of time. The progress of a case is endorsed on the file jacket, and the essential facts are set out in a summary written by a police officer involved in the case.

When you arrive, go to the CPS room where the files will be delivered to you if they are not there already. Defence advocates may be keen to speak to you about the case, eg, to ask whether you can serve advance disclosure. If you are ready ahead of 10 am then it will help them if you make yourself available as early as possible.

What if ...?

• *Your case is not listed?*

There may be a number of reasons why your case is not listed. Your client may only recently have been arrested and their name may simply not yet have been put on the court list. Sometimes the court will end up with up to four lists, each one adding a few more cases that have come to the court's attention as a result of the police having recently arrested people. The cases that involve recent arrests tend to be heard in the courts with the secure docks – normally Court 1. The usher of Court 1 would be a good place to start in trying to find your case.

If the usher(s) cannot help, you need to find the 'listing office'. Find out from the office which court the case will be heard in and inform the usher dealing with that court. You may be told that you have the wrong day or that you have arrived in the morning for a case listed in the afternoon. In the latter situation, wait around or go away and come back later. If you have the wrong day, there is nothing you can do except to make a note of the correct day. If you are counsel, telephone your instructing solicitor and explain the situation. You may want to consider charging for your wasted time and expenses. If you are at the wrong court, your clerk or your own office can find out where you ought to be. Make a decision as to whether it is feasible to make your way to the correct court. If so, proceed as quickly as possible, following the guidelines regarding arriving late (see Chapter 1).

• *Your client fails to arrive?*

See 'Warrants for non-attendance' (Chapter 7).

• *Your case is called and you are not ready?*

If your case is called, you must attend court. Benches are used to hearing advocates ask for more time so don't worry about asking. It is quite improper to be forced to proceed when you are not ready. Some tribunals, particularly District Judges, may require an explanation as to why you are not ready. They can show impatience, but ultimately there is little that they can do other than try to hurry you up. If you received instructions late in the day, or if your client arrived late, or if it was very hard to find a moment to talk to the prosecutor, then simply explain that this is the case, and ask for however long you need.

You may need to ask the bench to rise so that you can speak to the prosecutor. This is perfectly acceptable to ask for, so long as you have made all reasonable efforts to see the prosecutor before the list started.

3 Courtroom basics and etiquette

Inside the courtroom

Magistrates' courts can be very crowded and full of people, some of whom you may want to talk to before your case is heard, for example the prosecutor and the probation officer. As well as knowing where you should sit (and where you should not sit) it is also important to know where these other people will be sitting (see Appendix 1).

In most magistrates' courts there are rows of seats in the middle of the courtroom, facing the bench (the raised dais where the magistrates sit), and rows at the side.

The clerk or legal adviser sits immediately in front of the magistrates facing the court.

The prosecutor will sit in the front row in the middle of the courtroom facing the bench, normally on the side furthest away from the dock. You will usually be able to recognise them by the large number of files on their desk.

The probation officer will sit near the front of the court in a row at the side. Defence advocates sit in the rows in the middle of the courtroom on the side nearer the dock, as near to the front as possible.

Defendants may wait in court until it is time for their case to be heard. They should sit at the back of the court until their case is called on and then come forward into the dock, unless they are not on bail. The dock (where the defendant sits throughout their trial) is often, in the newer courts, at the side of the courtroom against the wall and connected to the cells by a door. It is separated from the rest of the court by a wall or barrier. Some docks also have bars or security glass surrounding them. In some of the older magistrates' courts, the dock is in the middle of the court facing the magistrates.

Defendants who appear in answer to a summons (rather than in answer to bail) do not have to go into the dock. These defendants will sit behind their advocate. Summonses are served in minor cases, such as minor road traffic cases where there has been no arrest.

All witnesses (including the defendant) called, by either the Prosecution or the Defence, give evidence from the witness box at the front of the courtroom. The witness box is usually on the side of the court opposite the dock. In some of the older magistrates' courts there may be only one row in the middle of the courtroom facing the magistrates where the Prosecution will sit.

Defence advocates should wait in the rows to the side or at the back. When their case is called they should move to sit alongside the prosecutor.

The usher or list caller will generally sit in the back row, in the middle, or at the sides and towards the back, so that they can get in and out of court easily. You can move around or go in and out of court or talk to your client in court before your case is called, except when someone is taking the oath. Sit at the end of the row if you are going to be popping in and out of court, so as not to disturb the other advocates.

Etiquette

Every time you enter or leave court, remember to bow (in practice, no more than a nod) to the magistrates. Everybody in court stands when the magistrates enter or leave court. Technically, if your case is the last on the list, you should not leave the courtroom before the magistrates; wait until the magistrates retire or indicate that you need not wait. This is called 'addressing the court'.

You should always stand when addressing the court and when you are being addressed. Some prosecutors get very lazy about this and do not stand up if they think that the exchange with the bench will be short. This is considered bad etiquette. Youth court proceedings may provide an exception and the practice may be for advocates to remain seated.

The tribunal: lay magistrates and District Judges

There are many differences between lay magistrates and District Judges. Your advocacy will need to adjust accordingly. District Judges will not require long expositions on the law relating to most common offences. They work much more quickly than lay magistrates and will not tolerate their time being wasted. They may also interrupt you more than lay magistrates. Lay magistrates rise a great deal to discuss matters before reaching their decision. Some benches and District Judges may view certain offences more seriously than other benches and District Judges. Find out from colleagues if your tribunal is known to be particularly harsh with cases like yours.

Also, if you get to court in plenty of time, take a few minutes to sit in and observe how the tribunal is dealing with other cases. As well as getting a feel for the tribunal and its mood, you may also be alerted to any peculiar local practices. It is also quite a good idea to ask someone in the advocates' room about a District Judge's reputation. Some District Judges have very distinct personalities, and it is well worth knowing all that you can find out about them.

Forms of address

There is an ancient distinction between the modes of address used by barristers and those used by solicitors. The distinctions seem hierarchical and uncomfortable, and many people disregard the rules, but the practices are meant to be as follows.

If you are counsel, you refer to all tribunals as 'Sir' or 'Madam'. If you have a District Judge, this is easy since you only have one person to address. If you have a lay bench, you address the chair of the bench alone. You may wish to include the other magistrates from time to time by referring to them as 'your colleagues' when addressing the chair, eg:

> Madam, have you and your colleagues had the opportunity to read the pre-sentence report?

Further to that, you should address opponents who are solicitors as 'my friend' and opponents who are barristers as 'my learned friend'.

If you are a solicitor, the convention is that you address a bench of magistrates as 'your worships' and a District Judge as 'Sir' or 'Madam'. It seems to matter little if you feel uncomfortable with 'your Worships' and opt for 'Sir' and 'Madam' throughout. I have never heard of a solicitor being criticised for using 'Sir' and 'Madam' to a lay bench, although the convention used to be that this was the form of address reserved for barristers. Further to that, the convention is that you refer to other solicitors as 'my friend' and barristers as 'my learned friend'. In practice, the terms are used with little consistency.

The clerk of the court is normally called the 'learned clerk', although the position is not so clear now that clerks are formally called 'legal advisers'. It is not clear whether advocates will adopt the expression 'legal adviser'; both forms of address are acceptable.

The usher is not referred to as 'learned'.

There is a tradition of avoiding the word 'you' when referring to a judge or magistrate. This does not, however, need to be followed to the letter. The reason for the custom is simply that in some circumstances it can sound too familiar and direct to use the word 'you'. For example 'will you please grant the defendant bail?' sounds too personal a request. An advocate should use the third person or address the court, for example:

Might I ask that *the court* grant the defendant bail?

There is, however, no absolute prohibition on addressing the tribunal with the word 'you'. It would be perfectly polite and acceptable to ask of a bench:

Sir, might I ask if you and your colleagues have had the opportunity to read the pre-sentence report?

This is far easier and more natural than asking, 'Have Sir and Sir's colleagues had the opportunity to read the pre-sentence report?' By starting a sentence with 'Sir' the advocate can show due respect and it is not necessary to use awkward forms of address in the third person.

Introductions

It is formal etiquette to introduce the parties in a case, but in practice this has almost completely ceased. One reason is that the prosecutor is usually the standing prosecutor for the day, and it would be unusual to reintroduce themselves over and over again. Advocates come in and out on something of a conveyor belt and introductions are rarely attempted.

The exception comes at trial. You should introduce the parties at the outset of a trial, so that the bench knows who is appearing and whom they represent.

The correct approach is that the person doing the introducing does not introduce his or her own name (the usher passes slips with the names to the bench), but merely says, 'I appear for the Crown/Defence in this case, and my friend/learned friend, Mr/Mrs/Miss/Ms Bloggs, appears for the Defence/Crown'. Note that first names should not be used, and, if you are introducing a female opponent, it would be advisable to ask if she wishes to be referred to as a Miss, Mrs or Ms.

4   Getting a representation order (legal aid)

The system of funding criminal cases has recently been reviewed. The old system was called 'legal aid' and you will still hear people talk about legal aid since this was the system for so long. However, now the courts talk about 'public funding' and if the court agrees that a case should be publicly funded, the court will issue a 'representation order' (RO). Applying for the order is a significant act and, if you do not use enough skill, you won't be paid!

Where to find the forms

The form on which you make the application for public funding is called 'Form A'. There is no set rule as to where you will find a Form A. The best place to ask is at the general office. Some courts have clearly marked offices that deal with public funding, although many of these are still called the 'legal aid office'. The other possible sources of the forms are the usher or list caller, the advocates' room, or in the courtroom itself. In short, the forms could be anywhere! The best thing is to ask other lawyers if it is not obvious.

Applying for a representation order

Application must be made on a Form A. Although oral applications are permitted (see later), a Form A must still be submitted with the oral application.

Your application will either be considered by a legal adviser or a delegated member of the court's administrative staff known as an 'appropriate officer'.

The first thing you need to make sure is that the form is filled in correctly and that it is legible (legal advisers and other appropriate officers will return forms or even refuse to grant representation if they cannot read them).

Make sure that you have filled in all the sections correctly and that you have got the form signed.

One area that applicants often get wrong is in the completion of the case details. Many courts only consider the grant or refusal of representation on what is written on the form so it is vital that all relevant information is included. Also, the appropriate officer will not grant separate representation without details of the conflict between any co-accused.

Section 5 of the application form is the most important section from an advocate's point of view. It is headed 'Reasons for wanting a right to representation'. In basic terms, you have to show that the case is sufficiently serious for the case to merit having legal representation. This is called 'the interests of justice test'.

The interests of justice test

This test is divided into a number of sub-criteria where the Defence seeks to argue the merits of having a lawyer instructed in the case. What follows is a review of each of the individual criteria that make up the interests of justice test.

- *Section 5a – likelihood of deprivation of liberty*

This is the criterion by which those defendants who face losing their liberty can apply for funding. On the face of it, this is the simplest ground for arguing that your client should have an RO: it certainly is the strongest.

This issue falls into two parts. First, the defendant might lose their liberty because they are not granted *bail*. So, for example, the defendant may be a routine shoplifter who has a poor record of previous offending and is at risk of not being granted bail, although the final sentence might only be a fine. It would be possible to argue that the defendant has a right to be funded since the funding is for the proceedings as a whole, which includes bail, for which the defendant may lose their liberty. If the police have denied bail, and you are filling in the form whilst your client is in the cells, you have a good chance of securing an RO. Fill the order in before you make the bail application. Then you can put on the form 'defendant is currently in custody', which is more persuasive than if he has just been granted bail and you have to enter, 'defendant was, until recently, in custody'.

The second part to answering section 5a is whether the *sentence* may result in a loss of liberty. This will depend on the case in question. Advocates, therefore, need to be aware in general terms of sentencing guidelines for the case from the very outset. These are helpfully dealt with in *Blackstone's Criminal Practice* (2003, Oxford: OUP), *Thomas on Sentencing* and the Magistrates' Association guidelines (which can be found in *Stone's Justices' Manual,* 2003, London: Butterworths).

Look out for specific types of cases where custodial sentences are routinely passed in magistrates' courts; these include assault on a police officer and driving whilst disqualified.

Take care in your application. Some offences, which in your opinion carry a risk of custody, may in fact not have the 'real and practical risk of imprisonment or other form of deprivation of liberty' (which is the test the appropriate officer will apply) in the light of recent guidance on sentencing. Theft from an employer is one prime example. The case of *R v Kefford* [2002] All ER (D) 37 makes it clear that a community penalty is the starting point for this type of offence.

A community penalty is not a deprivation of liberty for the purposes of the grant of representation (*R v Liverpool City Magistrates ex p McGhee* [1993] Crim LR 609).

Avoid contradicting yourself. Advocates can be seriously embarrassed if they have indicated on Form A that the defendant will probably receive a custodial sentence, but then submit in court that a custodial sentence would be entirely inappropriate. Whilst it is important make a strong case for the granting of funds, advocates must be very careful to be honest and realistic.

It is important to note here that if the defendant is going to elect trial at the Crown Court, the grant of representation is not automatic. An election does not make an offence more serious and the test applied does not change.

If there is a risk of a hospital order, or if the defendant is to be deported then representation should be granted.

- *Section 5b – breach of other sentences*

This criterion really follows on from the last. In considering the likelihood of the defendant losing their liberty, the advocate needs to consider whether a new conviction will put the defendant in breach of any other sentences. This could happen if there is an active conditional discharge, or an active suspended sentence. These extant sentences will need to be dealt with if a new conviction is registered during the active period of the conditional discharge or suspended sentence. An advocate may argue under section 5b that the combination of cases that will be dealt with at sentence would put the defendant at risk of custody.

It is, therefore, crucially important to look at the previous convictions of the defendant to check if there are any outstanding conditional discharges or suspended sentences. There may not be a record of the previous convictions available early on in a case. In this event, the advocate will have to make do with asking the defendant what the position is in relation to any past sentences and hope that the defendant is able to recall!

This section must also be considered if the defendant is in court for breach of a community penalty. Representation is likely to be granted if the Prosecution (which in the case of a breach could be the probation service, the youth offending team or the curfew monitoring service) is asking for the order to be revoked and the defendant to be re-sentenced. It is, therefore, important to ask the prosecutor before you fill in the form. If only a disciplinary breach is being dealt with, a grant is unlikely.

- *Section 5c – loss of livelihood*

A defendant may be eligible for funding if the proceedings might entail him losing his livelihood.

It may seem unpalatable to think that some people have more to lose by a conviction than others, but that is what is under consideration in section 5c. If the defendant is in the armed services, for example, a conviction for theft or violence could lead to the collapse of a career. The fact of a conviction might not really affect some people who are out of work (but see section 5d, below), or self-employed, whereas the simple fact of the conviction itself will change the lives of some others. If the defendant stands to lose his livelihood if convicted, it is possible that the court would think to provide publicly funded representation so as to afford the defendant all possible protection.

In road traffic cases where the defendant is likely to be disqualified from driving as a result of the offence and lose his livelihood because of the ban it is *unlikely* that representation would be granted under this heading. However, if you have a good argument for 'special reasons' the question of the grant of representation will be considered in a more favourable light.

- *Section 5d – damage to reputation*

If the defendant holds a job or undertakes voluntary work that relies upon having a particular reputation, and is charged with an offence that would cause *serious* damage to his reputation, representation may be granted. The important word in this section is *serious* and if you wish to rely on this ground for the grant of the RO you need to argue what is special about the defendant and why either a conviction or a particular sentence would seriously damage their reputation.

It is worth noting that social status is *not* to be taken into account. Reputation is a question of good character, including honesty and trustworthiness. Also, the ground is concerned with the penalty that the defendant may be subject to and there is nothing to stop an advocate arguing the need for an RO because the defendant needs expert mitigation to lower a sentence and therefore avoid suffering any stigma.

- *Section 5e – a substantial question of law is involved*

This is where an advocate would argue that the case in hand needs a lawyer because there is an issue that is too legally complex for an unrepresented person. A classic example would be where there is an alleged confession in interview, but there is an available argument that the interview is inadmissible. It would be hard for an untrained defendant to argue the point as competently as a lawyer. Any case where there is an issue of police procedure, and a point to be taken under the Police and Criminal Evidence Act 1984 (PACE), might attract public funding under this head.

Advocates must be prepared to cite any case law if they wish to rely on the section 5e criterion and need to remember that the question of law must be substantial. The criterion can still apply where the defendant pleads guilty. A classic example is laced drinks in cases of driving with excess alcohol where expert evidence needs to be sought even where a guilty plea is anticipated.

Other 'questions of law' that might arise could include issues under the Human Rights Act 1998. However, if you raise human rights points in this section you must include a reference to any European case law you are relying on.

It is important to try to read as much about the case as possible before filling in Form A so that any issues of law can be identified. Look out for any evidence that the Crown seeks to rely on which could be argued as being inadmissible. For example, in charges relating to domestic disputes, it is often the case that the complainant relates to past bad behaviour of the defendant. If this evidence could be ruled inadmissible after legal argument as evidence of past bad character, then this should be raised in support of your application under section 5e.

If the defendant is charged with complex offences, do not use this section to say that advice as to the *correct plea* is needed because of the complexity of the charges. Advice as to plea is almost never a substantial question of law.

- *Section 5f – ability to understand proceedings*

The State does not only have to pay for a defence advocate, it also has to pay for the Prosecution and for the court. Therefore, there is a premium on cases running efficiently and smoothly, and this may not happen if the defendant is weak at English or is disadvantaged in some other way in terms of participating in proceedings.

It can take hours to take even basic instructions from some defendants. If an RO has been granted, the State is only paying for the advocate's time. If the defendant was to go into court, and it took the court as much time to understand the defendant (and vice versa), the State will end up paying for all the court time, and indeed the waiting time of all the lawyers waiting on the court. For the sake of saving money and for expediency, it is plainly better to pay for the lawyer to do all the hard work in taking instructions and giving advice.

If the defendant does have difficulties of language, comprehension or other disadvantage, this should be explained in section 5f, and you should give the court some indication of the additional difficulties it will be taking on if it does not fund a lawyer in the case.

If an advocate seeks to rely on a mental or physical disability, the clerk/legal adviser or appropriate officer would want confirmation that the condition would actually impact upon the case. For example, do not simply say that the defendant is dyslexic. The condition may not prevent him from being able to present his own case; it depends on the complexity of the case and the severity of the condition. Medical reports may help establish a genuine need for representation and advocates should consider supplying some form of evidence of the condition and its effects if the application is to be successful under this criterion.

- *Section 5g – tracing witnesses*

It may be that the case involves an incident that occurred in a public place and that some investigation would turn up more witnesses or other evidence. This job is more likely to be accomplished in the interests of justice if it is performed by lawyers than by an unrepresented defendant. A member of the public would prefer to be asked to make a statement in a solicitor's office than be quizzed by a defendant. This may be so even if the defendant and the witness know one another. For example, if the potential witness is also the defendant's boss, it would be much less awkward for all concerned if solicitors were involved. In the interests of justice, a fair and professional statement should be taken, rather than the defendant trying to gather evidence on their own behalf. Do not forget to provide details of the witness in the application.

- *Section 5h – expert cross-examination*

When filling in the form, defence lawyers will need to envisage if there is likely to be a trial and what sort of form that trial might take. The court is unlikely to be much assisted by pantomime cross-examination ('oh yes you did', 'oh no you didn't!') and, depending on the complexity of the issues, there may be a need for a lawyer to handle the trial.

Sometimes the issues in a case are quite straightforward and little cross-examination is required. Take, for example, a case of shoplifting where the defendant accepts that he removed an item from a store, but says that he simply forgot that he had the item, and that he was not dishonest. Putting this defence does not require much, if any, cross-examination. In these circumstances, there is no particular need for the services of a lawyer (all else being equal). On the other hand, the nature of a defence may be such that the case will be won or lost on the cross-examination of a witness. In section 5h you might argue that it would be in the interests of justice to have the case run by an expert in the art of cross-examination rather than leaving the trial issues in the hands of the defendant.

This section is concerned with the expert cross-examination of a witness, not the cross-examination of an expert witness.

All police officers have some training in giving evidence and it may be hard for an unrepresented defendant to 'hold his own' with a police officer. If the case concerns a substantial issue involving the police it may be open to argument that expert cross-examination is required.

- *Section 5i – someone else's interests*

The 'someone else' is usually the alleged victim, and the point of this section is to protect victims who would be traumatised by facing the defendant in court.

If the defendant is pleading not guilty, then two classic examples under this heading arise. These are domestic violence and harassment. It will normally be sufficient to state that it is not appropriate for the defendant to cross-examine the alleged victim because of the nature of the offence. There may be other cases where it would not be appropriate for the defendant to cross-examine a witness and this is the paragraph to argue this point. For example, it may not be appropriate for a 20-year-old defendant to cross-examine a 60-year-old witness as the communication between them may be awkward. Take care to make the reasons clear.

Also you should consider whether or not your client is prohibited from cross-examining the alleged victim by any statutory bar. Examples are ss 34 (sexual offences) and 35 (child complainants) of the Youth Justice and Criminal Evidence Act 1999.

Representation is *not* normally granted on the grounds that it is in the interests of the defendant's family or children.

- *Section 5j – other factors*

This section is for you to add any other information not covered anywhere else in section 5 which you feel is relevant. For example, the defendant might be aggressive towards authority and be likely to be disruptive in the court if he is not represented.

Do not state that because a lawyer will represent the Prosecution, the defendant should be represented citing the Human Rights Act 1998 and 'equality of arms'. Your application is likely to be returned with the request that you provide all relevant case law to support that assertion.

Making an oral application

The preferred method of applying for an RO is in writing. This is not the only way, however. Advocates are entitled to apply directly to the bench. In general terms, it seems to be harder for benches to refuse an advocate face to face than it is for a clerk or legal adviser to refuse an application in writing. The only problem about applying directly to benches is that it infuriates the clerk/legal adviser who will try very hard to tell you that you are not entitled to apply in this way, or that it is improper. In any event, the clerk/legal adviser will not like the fact that you are going over their head and asking the bench directly.

There may be a good reason for asking the bench directly, which the clerk/legal adviser may appreciate once a proper explanation is offered. For example, it may be that the defendant is rather hard to deal with, and that your view is that the court should grant an RO on the basis that it is hard for the defendant to engage in proceedings (section 5f or 5j on Form A). This may be hard to express on the form, but once the court has seen the defendant in court, it will be plain why the court would need to have somebody looking after the defendant! You could, for example, phrase the application like this:

> Sir, I apologise for applying for a representation order orally and not in writing, but the court has now had the opportunity to see at first hand the difficulties that the defendant faces in engaging in these proceedings, and it is therefore easier for the court to appreciate why it is that granting a representation order would best serve this defendant, the court and the interests of justice.

There may be other reasons why the application is best made orally. For example, there may be a particular complexity in the case that would require more space to explain than the form provides. It may also be that the court hearing will inform the bench about the case, and it would seem to be a waste not to use that knowledge of the case to effect. Some bail applications will entail considerable information being put before the bench by both the Prosecution and Defence. You might say:

> Madam, you have just heard a substantial amount about this case, and whilst I know that the courts do prefer applications for public funding to be made on paper, I wonder if it would be improper to raise the matter orally since you have just had the opportunity of hearing and assessing this case in rather more detail than I am able to help the court with on Form A?

Do not forget, however, that you must still complete a Form A because the court needs it. Form A contains details about the defendant and the solicitor to whom representation is to be granted, and needs to be endorsed if the defendant goes to the Crown Court.

In summary

- Make sure the form is filled in legibly and all sections are completed.
- Make sure the defendant's details are correct and the form is signed.
- If charges are altered, ask for the new matters to be endorsed on the RO.
- If the defendant is sent or committed to the Crown Court ask for the RO to be extended and get a Form B.

What if ...?

- *The Prosecution changes the charge against the defendant?*

For example, representation is granted for a s 3 public order offence and the Prosecution, after reviewing the file, asks for a s 4 to be put in its place.

Technically, the RO is granted only for the original charge and if the charge is withdrawn the court could remove the order. The simple solution is to ensure that the court adds the new offence *before the original charge is withdrawn,* and make sure that the clerk/legal adviser marks the court file to this effect. If you follow this procedure, the RO will cover the new charge.

- *The magistrates decide to commit the defendant for sentence?*

Do not forget to ask for the RO to be extended to the Crown Court and ask the clerk/legal adviser for a Form B. Form B is the statement of means form that must be completed by all defendants in the Crown Court. (The clerk/legal adviser is in fact under an obligation to serve Form B and endorse Form A to the effect that it has been served.) Failure to get the RO extended at this stage is not fatal as you can apply to the Crown Court for it, but it is easier to get it extended at the magistrates' court.

- *The defendant is committed for trial to the Crown Court?*

Do not forget to ask for the extension of the RO and ask for Form B whilst the case is still at the magistrates' court.

- *The defendant faces an indictable only offence and is sent to the Crown Court under s 51?*

Make sure that the RO was a 'through order'. If it was not, ask for the extension of the RO to the Crown Court. The advocate simply asks in court whether the order is a 'through order' and asks for the extension if it is not.

- *The defendant wants to lodge an appeal from the magistrates' decision?*

Although the magistrates' court has power to grant representation for an appeal to the Crown Court, you should apply to the Crown Court for representation on an appeal.

- *You are sent to court on a case where public funding is not appropriate?*

This is an occupational hazard. Pupil barristers may come across unscrupulous firms that send work to chambers knowing full well that the chances of the case attracting public funding are next to zero. The firm would like to offer representation to the client to foster good relations in the hope that the client will use that firm in the future. If this is the position that you face, the best thing to do is to submit Form A and represent the client regardless. If you do a good job, it is possible that you too will benefit if the client commits a more serious offence in the future and wants you to represent them again. You might want to have a word with the clerks and just mention that the solicitors are sending in work with no prospect of getting paid.

- *You go to court and find out that the application for an RO has been refused?*

If only a written application has been made, the advocate can still make an oral application to the court (see above). If that application fails, the advocate, however, would be entitled to walk away. Most advocates would stay and do their best for the sake of good relations with the client.

- *The defendant has no money to get home?*

One option is to ask the court for payment of the defendant's fare out of the poor fund or poor box. Most courts have a small amount of money to give away for just this sort of problem.

5   First appearances – asking for disclosure

A first appearance, as the name suggests, is the first time a case is brought to court. It will normally follow an arrest and, if the matter is serious enough for the police to withhold bail, the first appearance will be at the next sitting of the court. Hence if someone is arrested and charged overnight, they should be brought to court later that same morning.

The first appearance is often simply a matter of (1) getting a representation order (RO), (2) adjourning so that you can receive and consider disclosure and (3) applying for bail if the defendant was arrested and held in custody.

In more simple cases, it is possible that the disclosure is ready, and the case can go all the way through plea and on to sentence if the plea is guilty. For simpler cases where the defendant is on bail, see the section below called '"Neary" courts' (p 36).

This chapter will look at adjourning for disclosure to be made and/or considered. Disclosure and the rules concerning disclosure are discussed in more detail in Chapter 13. In general terms, 'giving disclosure' or 'giving advance information (AI)' or 'advance disclosure (AD)' really just means that the Prosecution will give the Defence the statements of the witnesses who will be called to prove the charge.

Categories of offences and disclosure

The category of offence is the primary factor in determining the defendant's right to see the case against them. There are three categories of cases:

- *Indictable only offences*

This simply means the offence is always regarded as too serious for the magistrates' court, and the magistrates *must* send it *forthwith* to the Crown Court. Examples of indictable offences are murder, rape, s 18 grievous bodily harm, robbery, some serious firearms offences, perjury, and causing death by dangerous driving. If the offence charged is an indictable only offence, there will be little to do at the first appearance other than collect any disclosure there may be and consider the position with regard to bail.

* *Either way offences*

Either way offences are so called because they can be dealt with either in the Crown Court or the magistrates' court. The great majority of cases are either way, including almost all thefts and almost all offences of violence. If the case is an either way offence, the Defence is entitled to AD. You need to find the prosecutor as early as possible and see if they have any statements ready for you. If they do not, you should ask for an adjournment.

If there is no disclosure available at the first appearance and the defendant is in custody (and you are trying to prepare a bail application), you may find that some prosecutors are prepared to show the Defence the summary of the case. This is the summary that the police prepare for the prosecutors. If you want to make a bail application you really do need some information about the case and it is always worth asking the prosecutor if they will let you read the police summary.

So far as the form of the disclosure is concerned, the Crown Prosecution Service (CPS) has a habit of photocopying handwritten statements that are hardly legible. This is done so that the Prosecution can say that it has discharged its duty to disclose with all reasonable haste. The CPS is then very slow at producing typed statements if it ever does so at all. Even worse is the CPS's habit of not even getting witness statements from the police officers in the case, but instead giving the Defence a photocopy of the officer's little notebook. This is usually next to impossible to read. It seems that the Defence does not have the right to typed statements.

- *Summary only offences*

Summary offences are the offences that can only be heard in the magistrates' court. Most road traffic offences fall into this category. Importantly, common assault is summary only, and often cases that look as though they really should be charged as actual bodily harm (ABH) end up charged as common assault, so that they stay in the magistrates' court (where conviction rates are higher).

For summary offences the Defence is not entitled to disclosure. However, in many cases, if you ask nicely enough, the CPS will give you copies of the statements anyway. Basically, if the case is serious enough for you to have an RO, then it is serious enough for the interests of justice to demand that the Defence sees the statements in a case. If the prosecutor at court agrees that the Defence ought to have disclosure then you will need to adjourn for the CPS to send statements to the instructing solicitors. Make sure that the Prosecution is properly notified of the name and address of the solicitors acting in the case.

Making the application for an adjournment and disclosure

On a first appearance, advocates tend to ask for an adjournment simply because disclosure will not have been provided, or, if it has, it will probably only have been given to the advocate at court. The period of time that you ask for is usually quite standard – one week if the defendant is in custody, and two weeks if the defendant is on bail.

It is not inevitable that you will need to ask for an adjournment. If disclosure has been made and the case is simple, it may be that you have enough time to take the defendant through the statements and proceed to plea before venue.

Here are some sample applications:

Sir, this is the first listing of this case. The Defence has had no/very little disclosure. I apply for an adjournment for service of advance information.

Or:

> Sir, I have been handed some advance information only this morning. I request an adjournment to consider the papers properly, and take instructions regarding plea. [The statements are all handwritten and realistically there are too many statements to read them and take instructions on plea today.] Might I ask for a [7–14] days' adjournment?

Or:

> Sir, this is a summary only matter, but it is not an insignificant case [describe case], and therefore I have asked my friend/learned friend if he/she would be prepared to make voluntary disclosure which he/she has kindly agreed to. Might I ask for an adjournment of [14 days] for the Crown to provide some disclosure in the case?

'Neary' courts

A report was commissioned into how to speed up the court service. This report was called the 'Neary Report' being named after its chair, Martin Neary. The system that the report recommended also bears his name.

Different courts implement the Neary Report in slightly different ways, but the idea is as follows. The police or the CPS try to identify simple cases, where the defendant is on bail, and divide them into cases in which the defendants were 'caught red-handed' and will probably plead guilty, and those where the defendant's plea is likely to be not guilty, or the plea is hard to gauge.

The cases that are likely to result in guilty pleas are brought to court more quickly and the police try to disclose enough evidence quickly to encourage the defendant to plead guilty. The court may list a number of similar cases like this at one time. The court hearing these cases is often called an 'early first hearing court (EFH)'.

The practical effect is simply that if the case is listed for an EFH, the Prosecution should have statements ready to disclose and the hope will be that the matter can proceed to a plea on the first appearance. The bench will share the same hope and expectation. There is no compulsion to enter a plea at this first hearing if there is some reason why more time is needed to consider the evidence, but the likelihood is that the evidence is overwhelming and that the defendant may already have admitted the offence.

If the police and CPS are less confident that the defendant will simply plead guilty, the case may be listed in an 'early administrative court (EAC)'. The emphasis in this court will be on encouraging a plea to be entered (even if it is one of not guilty) and to make arrangements for trial.

Prosecutors

Prosecutors should, of course, attempt to secure a conviction, but in accordance with the code of conduct the attempt should not be at all costs, and it is submitted that the best practice for prosecutors is to aid disclosure whenever it is reasonably practicable to do so. If you can assist in giving information to the Defence then it will generally be helpful to do so. Do be careful *not* to disclose information that is clearly marked as being confidential.

If the Defence asks for disclosure in a summary only case and you take the view as prosecutor that the application has merit, the best course of action is either to make a quick phone call to the CPS lawyer (the phone numbers are usually clear in the papers) and ask for permission to disclose the information, or, if this is not practical, to adjourn the case and mark on the file that the Defence has requested disclosure. If the case has attracted public funding, make this clear on the file as the CPS will recognise that where the defendant is legally represented it makes sense to serve the papers on the Defence.

What if ...?

- *The defendant wants to enter a plea before there has been any disclosure?*

There is nothing wrong in entering a plea before disclosure has been made. If the defendant wants to plead guilty, then advise them that it would be very hard to change the plea back to not guilty if it transpires that the Prosecution actually has a very weak case. If the defendant wants to plead not guilty, and is certain of this plea, there is little harm in putting in the plea. A much fuller discussion on pleas follows in Chapter 10.

6   Bail

When to make a bail application (and when not to)

It is wise to discuss with the defendant whether he wants a
bail application to be made. Usually a defendant in custody
will want to apply for bail but there are exceptions. These are
dealt with below under the sections concerning taking
instructions on bail and advising on bail.

Limit to the number of bail applications

The general rule is that the Defence is entitled to two
applications for bail. It is rare not to make an application for
bail at the first opportunity even though at the first hearing
the Defence may not know a great deal about the
prosecution case. The true nature and extent of the case
against the defendant may only become clear over time, and
at the early hearings benches will tend to err on the side of
caution and allow the Prosecution some leeway in gathering
information against the defendant. Therefore, in the early
days of a potentially very serious offence the prospects of
bail are generally limited.

If the first application fails, a second application can be
made on the same grounds at the second or any other
subsequent hearing. After the two permitted applications are
exhausted, the only recourse is an appeal to the Crown
Court, or an application at the magistrates' court on the basis
of a *change in circumstances*.

Disclosure can take weeks or even months to complete
and over that time the goalposts can shift dramatically. For
example, a forensic test might come back 'negative' – ie, in
the defendant's favour. If there is a significant new piece of
information about a case, then the Defence can consider the
impact of this new information on the position in relation to
bail and launch a new application on the basis that there has
been a change in circumstances. There is no limit on how

many times there might be a change in circumstances in a case.

Terminology

The terminology in bail cases can be confusing. The confusion comes over the definition of the word 'remand'. When a case is adjourned, a decision needs to be made about what happens to the defendant. If the defendant was brought to the court *having been arrested*, the defendant will be 'remanded'. A remand is a requirement to return to court at the next hearing and to be subject to the Bail Act 1976. The remand can be in custody, or on bail. Either way, the *case* is *adjourned* and the *defendant* is *remanded* to the next court hearing.

The alternative situation is where the defendant was *not arrested*, but the Prosecution brings the case by way of *summons*. Almost all road traffic cases are instigated by summons. When the defendant attends court in answer to a summons, he is *not* bound by the Bail Act 1976 and the penalties in that Act for non-attendance. If the court decides to adjourn the case, the defendant can either be released and asked to attend on the next date (still not bound by the Bail Act 1976) or the court can decide to remand the defendant – ie, bring the Bail Act 1976 into the case and make the attendance at the next hearing mandatory and punishable.

A practical problem that arises is that most defendants misuse the word 'remand'. A remand is simply an obligation to surrender to the court in accordance with the Bail Act 1976 and the remand can be in custody or on bail. Many advocates and almost all defendants use a misleading shorthand. They use the word 'remand' to mean 'a remand in custody' and they use the expression 'being bailed' or 'getting bail' to mean a remand on bail. Hence a defendant will generally say, for example, 'will I get bail or be remanded?' What they mean, of course, is 'will the remand be on bail or in custody?'

Many defendants who are on bail will find that their hearts will miss a beat when a bench or District Judge says 'you will be remanded to (the next hearing)' because they will interpret this to mean that their bail is going to be withdrawn. Of more consequence to advocates conducting conferences with their clients is the warning that the expression 'you will be remanded' will be understood to mean that the remand will be in custody.

The next preliminary point about bail is that it always sounds as though it is a defence application, ie, it is the Defence that applies for bail. The terminology is negative to the extent that it conceals the fact that a defendant has a *right* to bail, and in many ways the better way to think of it is that the *Prosecution* makes an application for a remand into custody.

It is only because the defendant is actually in custody that an advocate talks about a bail application, ie, an application to change the status quo. Bear in mind though that it is for the Prosecution to discharge the burden of showing why bail should *not* be granted, rather than for the Defence to show why bail should be granted.

Can a defendant be remanded in custody for a non-imprisonable offence?

In general terms, if the defendant is charged with an offence for which he cannot be sentenced to a prison term, he does not have to be concerned about a remand into custody. *Only* if the defendant breaches bail in the proceedings can the court even consider a remand in custody.

Objections to bail

Some advocates are unclear about the distinction between the proper *objections* to the right to bail and the permissible *grounds* for believing that the objections are made out.

The *objections* to bail are limited. The primary trio of objections are that:

> The court has *substantial* grounds for believing that the defendant, if granted bail, would:

1. fail to surrender to custody; and/or

2. commit further offences whilst on bail; and/or

3. interfere with witnesses or otherwise pervert the course of justice.

The test is 'substantial grounds', and prosecutors often do not use the correct test and make submissions such as, *'the police have some concerns that ...'*. The test is a stringent one for the Prosecution. Expressions of concern are not enough.

The remaining objections to bail are less frequent but are as follows:

4. The Prosecution needs longer to ascertain the facts of the case (and a decision on bail must be put back).

5. Custody is necessary for the protection of the defendant.

6. The defendant is in custody already.

7. The defendant has already absconded in these proceedings.

Grounds

Having identified the objection(s) to bail, the Prosecution then needs to give the *grounds* on which the objection is based. The grounds can be diverse and numerous, but classic grounds include such things as:

- The nature and seriousness of the offence and the probable method of dealing with the defendant on sentence. The gravity of the offence is not in itself a reason for refusing bail. However, it is often argued that if a severe sentence is looming the defendant is likely to abscond.

- The defendant's character, antecedents, associations and community ties (including employment as well as family). A married defendant in employment who owns their own house is thought to be less likely to abscond than a single, unemployed defendant of no fixed abode.

- The defendant's previous record when granted bail. The previous convictions may show that the defendant has committed offences on bail in the past and/or that the defendant has failed to attend court in the past.

- The strength of the evidence against the defendant. The stronger the prosecution evidence, the greater the likelihood of conviction and, so it is thought, the greater the likelihood of the defendant absconding.
- Any other relevant reasons, including fears for the safety of prosecution witnesses known to the defendant and easily contactable by them.

Meeting objections to bail

Before the hearing, defence advocates should ask the prosecutor whether or not there are objections to bail. The prosecutor may then say that there are objections to bail based on any of the objections 1 to 7 listed above. Ask the prosecutor what grounds they are relying upon in support of the objection(s) so that you can prepare a submission to meet these objections once you get into court.

Discuss the objections to bail with the defendant. For example if they have breached bail in the past, find out what the circumstances were. It may be that they had a good reason and you can argue that it was an isolated incident that is unlikely to be repeated.

Check that you have an up to date copy of the defendant's antecedents (usually just called 'previous') and if you do not, ask the prosecutor for one. Do not rely on what the defendant tells you about their previous record unless you have to. Go through the record and in particular the circumstances of any similar offences to the present charge. If the defendant is denying the offence, check whether or not the defendant pleaded guilty to other offences in the past. If the defendant has always pleaded guilty in the past, he may be more credible in contesting the charges now.

Take the defendant's instructions about the offence with which they are charged and consider the strength of the prosecution evidence and the nature and seriousness of the allegations. You should also be clear about the defendant's present circumstances, such as family ties, responsibilities, employment and the possible effects of being remanded in custody. Try to take as detailed instructions from the defendant as possible.

Discuss conditions that could be attached to bail (see 'Conditions attached to bail', below). When you make your application you should deal with the objections raised and suggest conditions.

Do not discuss objections unless they are actually raised. For example, if the only objection is risk of absconding, then it is unnecessary to explore whether the defendant is likely to interfere with witnesses.

Although the court is obliged to accept the Prosecution's version of events for the purposes of determining bail, you can make clear to the court that the defendant denies what is being alleged.

Conditions attached to bail

If the Prosecution is objecting to bail, the defence advocate should think about offering to the court various conditions that could be attached to bail to meet those objections. Obviously defence advocates should first talk through suggested conditions with the defendant, as there would be no point in obtaining conditional bail with conditions that the defendant would not keep.

The following table shows various objections and suggests some conditions that might meet those objections.

Objections to bail	Suggested conditions
Failing to surrender to custody	**Residence**. This helps police, court and solicitors to know where D lives. It aids communication so that people can help remind D where he is supposed to be! Where D is of no fixed abode, talk to the probation officer and see if a bail hostel can be arranged.
	Surety. This is a sum of money, put up by D or someone known to D, which would be forfeited if D does not attend future hearings (see below, p 46, for how to do this).
	Reporting to police station (at some frequency between daily and weekly). This ensures that D does not leave the area. The police can keep track of D and remind them when they are next due in court.
	Surrender passport. D gives passport to police. Helpful condition if D has connections overseas.
Re-offending If offence committed at night.	**Curfew**. This simply means that D is not allowed out during the hours set down.
If the offence committed through drink.	**Ban on entering pubs** (often referred to as on-licence premises) or off-licence premises.
If offence is committed at a particular place or location.	**Ban on entering particular place or premises**. This can often apply to shoplifters who have favourite stores for stealing things.
Interference with witnesses	**Not to contact that witness directly or indirectly**. **Exclusion** – ie, not to come within distance X of witness Y.

D = the defendant

Sureties

A person who offers to stand as a surety does so with the obligation of ensuring the defendant's attendance at court. It is therefore important to establish what relationship the proposed surety has with the defendant, eg, relation, good friend or work colleague. When a defence advocate meets a possible surety they should find out how much money the surety would be prepared to offer, where that money is (eg, in a bank account), the relationship with the defendant and whether the surety has any previous convictions.

The surety must be aware that the money can be forfeited if the defendant fails to attend court. It is standard practice for the police to check whether the surety has previous convictions and, depending on the nature of the convictions, the prosecutor may object to the proposed surety. The money must be easily accessible, eg, in a bank or building society account.

If you are making a bail application and have a surety at court, you should, in your speech, inform the bench that the defendant's father/sister/friend, etc, is prepared to stand as surety in the sum of £x. If the court is prepared to consider granting bail subject to a surety, then at the end of your speech you will be asked to call the surety to the witness box.

Normally the defence advocate will question the person standing surety, but in some magistrates' courts the clerk/legal adviser or the District Judge will do this. The surety must be identified (name and address). Then the advocate should ask the surety what their relationship is with the defendant. The surety should be asked what sum they are prepared to forfeit, and the surety must confirm that they understand that this sum can be forfeited in whole or in part if the defendant does not attend in the future.

Applications to vary conditions

If, for example, the defendant has been granted conditional bail and one of the conditions imposed is that he resides with his girlfriend at her flat but subsequently the relationship breaks down, it will be necessary to apply to the court to vary the condition of residence. If he can give an alternative fixed address, eg, with his mother, there should be no problem in getting the condition varied. Be careful, however, if the condition has been imposed to exercise some control over the defendant. For example, if a young man who works in the family business has been granted bail on condition that he lives at home, a court may be reluctant to allow him, following an argument with his family and the termination of his employment, to live with a friend, especially if one of the reasons for imposing the original condition was to guard against him committing further offences.

Taking instructions on bail

Bail applications are enormously important to defendants and can really make a difference to how the defendant views his advocate. Good bail applications can help build a client base and prosperous legal careers. Here are some tips:

- Be practical. Push the defendant for conditions that would make it *safe* for them to have bail. Think about creative and practical solutions to the fears expressed by the Prosecution.

- Be realistic. Be very careful not to set defendants up to fail. If you have a chaotic client who takes drugs and misses every appointment they are ever given, a condition such as signing on at the police station every day is likely to land the defendant back in custody. It can be very damaging psychologically to be granted bail only to be taken back into custody for breach of a condition. Always be absolutely sure that the client understands what conditions you are going to offer on their behalf.

- Be tactically aware. With regard to whether you should be asking for bail at all, there are several things to remember. Clients always say that they want bail, but it is not *always* in their best interests to have it! The times when it is not in their interests are rare but important.

When it may be best to advise against making a bail application

- Time in custody before sentence can help the eventual sentence. Any time that a defendant spends in custody awaiting trial or plea counts towards any eventual sentence. Hence it is often the case that a spell in custody awaiting sentence makes it considerably easier to get a non-custodial sentence ultimately.

  For example, imagine that you represent a burglar. The defendant was, at the time of the offence, a heroin addict. They are in custody, and having a miserable time but are actually more or less clean of drugs. They are keen to receive a rehabilitation order for sentence. On the face of it the offence is too serious, and they are going to receive a custodial sentence. If, however, they can 'get some time under their belt' and come to the sentencing hearing having been in custody on remand for two or three months (equivalent to a four- to six-month prison sentence) then you have an outside chance of persuading the sentencing bench that a rehabilitation order *plus* the time already served *might* just be enough to mark the seriousness of the offence. Without the time already in custody, the court would not be able to pass a non-custodial sentence.

- Loss of privileges. The other issue is the loss of 'remand privileges'. Prisoners who have pleaded guilty or have been convicted go to different wings of the prison from the prisoners who have not yet been convicted. Prisoners who have not been convicted or pleaded guilty are called 'remand prisoners' and they have privileges that other prisoners do not.

  If it looks as if the defendant is destined for a prison sentence, then consider whether it is better for the defendant to serve some of the sentence with remand privileges rather than the whole of the sentence as a serving prisoner. If the defendant was remanded in custody and the plea held back as long as possible then the defendant can work off the sentence in much better conditions. However, watch out for losing credit (see Chapter 10).

It will make you look more streetwise if you can ask the defendant how important the 'remand privileges' are to them. You can then advise, where appropriate, that the defendant might be better in the long run if they remain in custody for the time being and serve some of their sentence with their privileges.

Getting the right pitch

The final important point to remember is that, for the purposes of bail decisions, all tribunals tend to work on the assumption that the defendant is guilty of the offence. The Defence may seek to challenge this assumption, but the best applications for bail are ones that can show that the defendant could be safely admitted to bail *even if* they are eventually shown to have acted in the way alleged by the Prosecution.

Whilst many defendants like it if their advocate protests their innocence at a bail application, it is less likely to be persuasive with the court. You need to have strong grounds to say that the prosecution case is doomed to fail before this becomes a meritorious approach to take.

Lord Archer was given bail in the face of overwhelming evidence of perjury for which he was sentenced to four years. The nature and seriousness of the offence and the strength of the evidence are only factors used in considering the likelihood of absconding, etc; they are not proper objections in their own right. It is worth explaining to defendants that bail applications are not mini-trials. It is generally more useful to look at how the defendant proposes to satisfy the court's doubts about good behaviour on bail than it is to try to convince the court that they are innocent.

Can bail be granted in the defendant's absence?

Yes. This is called 'enlarging' bail. Magistrates who have remanded a defendant can make further remands in their absence if they are unable to attend by reason of illness or accident. The remands may be in custody or on bail and, if in custody, may exceed eight clear days. If the defendant has been remanded on bail the court can, in the defendants absence, appoint a new time at which they are to appear.

The court may appoint a new time when the defendant does not appear and an explanation is given for non-appearance, which the court accepts. Alternatively, if the court does not accept the explanation, it may issue a warrant for the defendant's arrest.

Sometimes the court will list a case for a very short hearing, eg, to list a case for trial. It may be that there is little need to have the defendant present for this hearing. The Defence should ask that the defendant's presence be excused. If this is granted, then at the next hearing, when a date is set for the trial, the Defence simply needs to ask the court to enlarge the defendant's bail to the trial date.

What happens if the defendant has absconded?

See Chapter 7 on warrants.

Procedure for bail applications

First and foremost, the bench will need to know whether a bail application is going to be made. It is not compulsory, so you need to think whether you want to make one or not (see above). It is best to let the Prosecution know in advance, even if it is a quick whisper across the bench as the case is called in. Bail is normally the last issue dealt with in any hearing. Take the case as far as it can go and then mention the bail position at the end. If the Prosecution objects to bail it will then outline the facts of the offence and outline the objections. The Defence then makes the application for bail, responding to the objections made by the Prosecution.

Good bail applications will generally take each of the Prosecution objections in turn and answer them. Good practice would also be to look at the conditions that would satisfy the objection whilst you are dealing with that objection. Less effective advocates will simply make a speech about the defendant's circumstances, and list some conditions at the end, which really do not tie in logically. You should see the potential conditions to bail as a remedy to the concerns of the Prosecution about how the defendant will behave on bail.

Prosecutors

There should be information in the file that indicates the police and/or Crown Prosecution Service's (CPS) view about bail. The prosecutor's duty is to put these before the court. Be very careful about using the correct test for bail, which is that there are 'substantial grounds' for believing that one of the objections to bail is made out. Be careful not to confuse an 'objection' with a 'ground' for an objection. For example, a justified objection is that the defendant will fail to surrender. A ground for that objection is that the offence is serious in nature. It would, therefore, be wrong to seek a remand in custody merely on the basis that the offence is serious in nature. This is not a recognised objection to bail.

Many CPS lawyers use abbreviations when documenting bail, which can be confusing at first. Some familiar abbreviations used in relation to bail are:

FTA – Fail to attend

FTS – Fail to surrender

OOB – Offend/offence on bail

LFO – Likely further offences.

The police may have objections to bail, which could prove immaterial if the defendant was to offer the right condition. For example, if the defendant lives in a flat where there is known to be ready access to drugs locally, then the police may register an objection to bail on the basis of fear of further offending. At the hearing, the Defence may produce a different address to which the defendant could be bailed. Generally, the police like to check any address before they withdraw an objection to bail being granted. If a new address is offered, or indeed if the Defence have any seemingly good ideas about reducing the risk in giving the defendant bail, then speak to the police liaison officer at court and see what their view is. It may be that the objection can be withdrawn.

7   Warrants for non-attendance

What happens to a defendant who does not attend?

If you are defending and your client does not attend, there are three options available.

If you know the reason for the non-attendance and the reason is a good one, you might simply ask that the case is adjourned, and bail 'enlarged'. This just means that the defendant remains on bail as before, but with a duty to attend on the next hearing date. The court will send a letter to the address of the defendant advising of the new date. To have bail enlarged, you would normally need a letter from a doctor or some other strong evidence that the defendant is detained through no fault of their own.

The second and third options both relate to warrants for the arrest of the defendant. There are warrants 'backed for bail' and warrants 'not backed for bail'.

Warrants backed for bail

If a court issues a 'warrant backed for bail', what it is doing is putting out a warrant for the defendant to be arrested but not detained. The front of the warrant will specify that the defendant should be arrested for failing to appear, and the back of the warrant will say that the defendant should be allowed to stay on bail. The advantage of a warrant backed for bail, over simply enlarging bail, is that an officer will formally arrest the defendant and speak to the defendant face to face about the seriousness of having not attended on the last occasion and the need to come to court on the date specified on the warrant. The warrant backed for bail does not presume how the failure to appear will be dealt with – ie, the defendant could still be punished (see below).

Defence advocates will ask for a warrant backed for bail if there is some suggestion that the defendant's absence is explicable and for good reason. If there has been some terrible problem with the trains, for example, it would probably be wrong to assume that the defendant's absence is malicious.

If you do not know where the defendant is nor know why they have not attended you should always try to find out. It will be important to know if the defendant has a mobile phone, and to call it if there is one! If you do not have any details of the defendant's phone number, then call the solicitor's office and find out if anyone there can assist you.

Warrants not backed for bail

If you have not heard any reason why the defendant has not arrived, and steps have been taken to find out (eg, by calling them), then the usual order is a warrant not backed for bail. In this case, an officer will try to find the defendant, and, as and when this takes place, the defendant will be taken into custody and produced at a magistrates' court.

If an advocate has no reason to offer for why the defendant has not appeared, then it is not usual to oppose the Prosecution's application for a warrant not backed for bail. The advocate is quite entitled to say that they cannot assist the court with why the defendant has not appeared, and that the Defence has no applications or submissions to make. The Prosecution will ask for a warrant not backed for bail, which will be granted as a matter of course.

How long should an advocate wait for a defendant?

There is no set rule. If the defendant has a bad record of attending, you may take the view that it would be a waste of time to wait. There is always the chance that the defendant will arrive moments after you leave, but one has to draw the line somewhere.

The amount of time that you wait will depend on how busy the court is. It may be that you can sit waiting for hours before anyone really troubles you to ask if you are ready. On the other hand, the court may be impatient to start a trial and will want any other business finalised quickly.

Defendants are supposed to surrender to the court half an hour before the hearing. It is probably not worth worrying until the defendant is over half an hour late at which point you may begin to think about making some enquiries. Call any telephone numbers that you may have for the defendant. If you have no numbers, you should call the solicitor's offices to see if anyone there has a record of a number for the defendant.

Check very carefully that the defendant is not in the building. Check you are calling out the right name. It may be that you have shouted out the name, but your pronunciation is so bad that the defendant did not recognise your call as their name! Check routinely with the usher to see if the defendant has arrived and checked in without your noticing.

Also check that the defendant is not in custody. It is unlikely, but not impossible, that the defendant has been arrested recently and appears in custody without this information finding its way to you. Go to the cells and ask if the defendant is being held there.

The hearing when the defendant is brought to court after a warrant has been executed

When a defendant is arrested because of the warrant issued for a prior non-attendance, the procedure is called 'executing' the warrant. The defendant is produced at the court that is dealing with the substantive offence.

Failing to appear is a criminal offence (unlike breaching conditions of bail which is only punishable by removal of bail). The procedures for finding a defendant guilty of failing to attend (contrary to s 6 of the Bail Act 1976) are unusual.

It is up to the court to decide whether to initiate proceedings. What tends to happen in practice is that the bench will ask the defence advocate for an explanation for the non-attendance. The bench will usually make a decision there and then over whether to accept the reason. If the excuse is reasonable, then it may be that the matter will simply rest there without any action being taken in relation to the failure.

If the bench is not content to accept the explanation for not attending at face value, then there will need to be a hearing to determine whether the defendant is formally guilty of the Bail Act offence.

To avoid being found guilty of failing to appear, it is for the defendant to show 'reasonable cause' for failing to appear. Forgetting the date is not generally held to be a reasonable cause.

If the bench is not minded to accept the reason for the failure to attend on hearing just from the advocate, the next step is for the bench to ask the clerk/legal adviser to put the charge to the defendant. If the defendant has no good reason for failing to attend, then they must plead guilty to the offence. If the defendant thinks that there is reasonable cause (on advice from the advocate) then they should plead not guilty. The bench *can* hear the issue of the breach of bail there and then but better practice is to adjourn the issue to the conclusion of the proceedings (*Practice Direction (Bail: Failure to Surrender)* [1987] 1 WLR 79).

Considering bail after the execution of a warrant

The defendant may be granted bail again despite the problem that led to the issuing of the warrant, but it will not be easy. The Prosecution will rely on the objection of failure to surrender and the objection is likely to succeed.

It may be that the defendant accepts being guilty of failing to surrender but can argue through their advocate that the circumstances were isolated and unlikely to recur. It may be that the imposition of an additional condition of bail would remedy the defect that caused the failure in the first place. An example would be bailing a defendant to a more suitable address where it would be easier for the solicitors and the court to keep in contact. Another example would be bailing the defendant with an additional requirement to sign on at a police station so that the court proceedings could be kept uppermost in the defendant's mind.

Bail Act offences put pressure on defendants to plead guilty to the main offence

What often happens is that the defendant is charged with an offence that is not especially serious, but they fail to attend. The court removes bail and remands the defendant in custody. The Defence will frequently reconsider plea at this stage, the reason being that now that the defendant is destined to spend some time in custody there is little to be gained by going to trial. If the sentence would, ordinarily, be non-custodial or a custodial sentence of short duration, then there is a good chance that a greater penalty will be served awaiting the trial than would be passed after it. It is quite appropriate to ask the court for the soonest possible trial date, but if this date is more than a few weeks or so away, it may be worth talking to the defendant about their plea and seeing whether they really want to pursue a not guilty plea if waiting for the trial will now be in custody.

Trying the issue of whether the defendant had 'reasonable cause'

It is rare to have trials for Bail Act offences. The fact of the non-attendance speaks for itself. The defendant will already have been asked the reason for the absence and if the explanation was reasonable then no proceedings would have been brought.

On the occasions when there does need to be a hearing, one generally only hears from the defendant. The prosecution case will normally speak for itself and the defendant will admit that they were supposed to have attended on the date specified. The date to which the defendant is to be bailed is stated to the defendant in open court at the end of every hearing and the defendant is given a written bail notice indicating the return date.

Hence, usually a Bail Act hearing is simply a matter of hearing the defendant in the witness box explaining on oath why they failed to appear. The defence advocate would call the defendant, identify the defendant ('can you confirm your full name?') and then ask a few questions that allow the defendant to explain the matter. The Prosecution may ask some questions to test the credibility of what the defendant has said. The defence advocate may then address the bench on whether the bench would accept this explanation as being 'reasonable' in all the circumstances.

Sentencing a Bail Act offence

Where the defendant has pleaded guilty to failing to surrender, the best practice is to adjourn the sentence to the conclusion of the proceedings for which the bail was granted in the first place. This is because it is always best to look at sentencing in the round. In many cases the defendant will have lost bail because of failing to attend and so will already have paid a heavy penalty for the breach.

The maximum penalty in the magistrates' court is three months' custody and/or a fine of up to £5,000.

Bail Act offences are generally thought to be distinct from the main offence, and it would be quite normal for a bench to pass a consecutive sentence for the Bail Act offence. Defence advocates should deal with whether this would be appropriate in the case in hand. If bail has been refused as a consequence of the Bail Act offence then it would be normal to submit that this constitutes punishment enough. The bench will often pass a financial penalty with a period of custody in default of payment. As the defendant has been in custody already the sentence will have been completed. The other alternative is to pass a concurrent sentence.

Summary of procedure

When a defendant does not attend:

- The Defence should make enquiries to try to contact the defendant and find out why he has not attended.

- The Defence should wait a reasonable time and then notify the usher that the case is 'non-effective' because the defendant has not attended.

- When the case is called, the court will normally wait for the defendant – tell the court that the defendant is not here.

- The Defence explains any reason for the non-attendance if any reason is known.

- If the Defence has a reason for the non-attendance, the advocate should tell the court whether they are asking for bail to be enlarged or for the court to issue a warrant backed for bail. It is not appropriate to ask for these if the advocate has no instructions to explain the failure to attend.

- The court may make the order for the warrant without even consulting the prosecutor. If the prosecutor is asked, they are likely to ask for a warrant not backed for bail.

- The court will make an order enlarging bail or issuing a warrant.

- The defence advocate is then free to go.

When a defendant is arrested following the execution of a warrant:

- Normally the Defence will speak first to explain the reason for the defendant being produced in court.

- The Defence should tell the court when the defendant was supposed to attend court, explain that a warrant was issued, and say when the warrant was executed on the defendant.

- The Defence goes on to give an outline of any reason or excuse for the failure to attend.

- If there is a reason or excuse, the Defence asks the court not to initiate proceedings.

- If there is no reason for not attending, the Defence simply states that there is no reason for the defendant not having attended. It might be worth apologising on behalf of the defendant!

- The bench will then decide whether to put a charge of failing to attend to the defendant.

- The defendant pleads guilty or not guilty.

- The trial or sentence of the Bail Act offence should be adjourned to the conclusion of the main hearing.

- The court will then determine how to deal with bail for the next adjournment. The prosecutor will outline the details of the existing case and make representations about a remand in bail or in custody.

- The Defence will make a bail application if it wishes.

Prosecutors

The procedure outlined above should assist those prosecuting. The issue of whether proceedings should be brought for failing to attend is really a matter for the court, and it is submitted that it is proper for the Prosecution to take a neutral view. It is the court that decides whether to instigate proceedings, not the Crown Prosecution Service. 'Failure to surrender' means failing to surrender to the custody of the court, and it is the court that must determine whether the defendant has breached their obligation to the court. As prosecutor you should offer any assistance asked of you, but it is not appropriate actively to seek to take on this prosecution.

When a defendant denies that they are guilty of failing to surrender, any questions about the reasons put forward by the defendant are normally framed and put by the clerk/legal adviser. If you are prosecuting and you can think of a question that might assist the court in determining whether to believe the defendant, you may seek to help the court by putting a question to the defendant. Otherwise, leave it all to the court.

Prosecutors should, however, make representations about whether bail should be granted again in light of the failure to surrender.

8   Breach of bail conditions

What happens if a defendant breaches bail conditions?

This chapter covers what happens if a defendant breaches a condition of their bail. This is distinct from failing to surrender, which is not a condition of bail but a requirement in all cases where the defendant is remanded on bail.

First and foremost, it is not a criminal offence to breach a condition of bail. The only available sanction for breach of bail is loss of bail. There can be no additional or separate penalty.

It is open to a police officer to arrest somebody for breaching a bail condition or where there is suspicion that someone will breach a bail condition (s 7(3) of the Bail Act 1976). For example, if there is a condition of curfew from 9 pm and an officer sees the defendant queuing for a nightclub at 8.45 pm, it is not necessary to wait for the actual breach at 9 pm.

Following the arrest, the defendant must be brought before the magistrates' court as soon as is practicable and at least within 24 hours.

The hearing that follows is to determine whether a breach has taken place and to decide on whether the defendant can be safely readmitted to bail or not. The first step is for the clerk/legal adviser to ask the defendant whether they admit or deny that there was a breach (or would have been a breach) of the condition concerned. The defendant then either admits or denies the breach of the bail term. This is not a 'plea' as such, since there is no criminal charge, but it has much the same effect, since a denial would trigger a hearing of the issue.

Procedure if the breach is admitted

If the breach is admitted, the Prosecution will be asked for its views on whether bail should continue. If the breach is serious the Prosecution is likely to seek a remand in custody, even if the Prosecution consented to bail earlier. For example, if the case is a common assault of a partner and the defendant has been seen loitering outside the 'victim's' place of work despite being bailed to stay away, the Prosecution would re-evaluate its concern about interference with witnesses. However, if the breach is less serious (eg, spending a night at a friend's house when the defendant was supposed to live and sleep each night in their own house) then the Prosecution may have no objections to bail being renewed.

The breach may have taken place because of a change in circumstances and the remedy would simply be to change or remove the condition. This can happen when a defendant is on curfew but is offered shift work at night, or where an address that was suitable becomes impractical for some reason. The Defence simply needs to approach the issue with common sense. The hearing is really just another review of bail.

If the defendant had difficulty with a bail condition, they should have notified their solicitors so that an application could have been made to vary bail before the problem arose. The defendant will be criticised to some extent for breaching bail regardless of whether there was a good reason. The court will regard a defendant more cynically if there has been a breach in the past, especially if the breach could have been foreseen but nothing was done to vary bail.

The summary of the procedure on an admitted breach is:

- Case is called on.

- Prosecutor explains briefly the reason for the defendant being arrested.

- The defendant is asked to admit or deny breach.

- If the breach is admitted, the Prosecution is to explain its position in relation to continued bail.

- Defence to make representations about continued bail.

Procedure if the breach is denied

If the breach is denied, the issue of the breach should not be adjourned but should be dealt with there and then. Ideally, the officer involved in the arrest should be present at court since his or her evidence may be disputed. In most cases there is no dispute about why the defendant was arrested for breach (or anticipated breach), and the hearing is for the defendant to explain themselves.

An example would be a defendant who is bailed to observe a curfew and reside at a certain address. The police attend at the house after the curfew has started and ring the bell. There is no answer. The next day the police arrest the defendant for breach of the curfew condition. There is no real dispute that the police officer attended and rang the bell; consequently the evidence need not be given live by the officer but can be read out by the prosecutor. The defendant would then simply need to explain (probably best on oath) why they deny the breach (eg, that they were indeed at home but sleeping heavily and never heard the bell).

As this hearing is not a trial, there are no rules of evidence. The Prosecution can adduce evidence as it wishes and the rules of hearsay, etc, are not applicable. The hearings are often rather haphazard and the procedures are flexible.

The procedure for a contested breach of bail condition hearing should be along the following lines:

- Case is called on.

- Prosecutor explains briefly the reason for the defendant being arrested.

- The defendant is asked to admit or deny breach.

- If the breach is denied, the Prosecution is asked to give its grounds for alleging the breach of bail condition. The Prosecution calls an officer or reads their statement.

- If an officer is called (because of a dispute over the evidence), the Defence can cross-examine.

- Defence should call the defendant. The Court has discretion to have the defendant sworn. Defendant asked in-chief to explain why they deny breaching bail.

- Prosecution can cross-examine the defendant.

- Defence might ask to make a speech before the bench considers its view, but this is very unlikely to be necessary.

- Bench decides whether there has been a breach or not.

- If breach found *not* to have occurred, then the defendant *must* be re-bailed on the same terms unless the Defence asks for a variation.

- If breach *is* found to have occurred, the Prosecution is asked to make representations about whether the next remand should be on bail or in custody.

- Defence should respond to the Prosecution's representations.

- Bench to determine whether to grant bail or not.

9   Plea before venue (PBV)

This section deals only with the mechanisms for entering the plea in court. The next chapter is dedicated to considering what plea to enter and some associated tactical considerations.

The decision on where to hear a case is only relevant to those cases that can be heard 'either way' (ie, by the magistrates' court or by the Crown Court). Summary only cases can only be heard by the magistrates' court, and indictable only offences must be sent to the Crown Court. See Chapter 5.

Many cases are 'either way'. *Blackstone's* (2003, Oxford: OUP) will indicate the classification of each offence, but in general terms all thefts (not involving motor vehicles) are either way, as are all assaults save common assault and assaulting a police officer in the execution of their duty. Public Order Act offences are summary if they are charged as s 4 or s 5: they are either way if charged as s 2 or s 3. Most driving offences are summary only. Driving whilst disqualified and drink-driving offences are all summary only. Dangerous driving is either way. Most of the main offences regarding weapons are either way offences: possession of a bladed article is summary only.

Terminology

There are a number of phrases used to describe the same thing. Deciding the correct court in which to hear a case can be described in any of the following terms:

* deciding *venue*;
* deciding the appropriate *forum*;
* determining the *mode of trial*.

Overview of how the venue for a case is determined

In the 'old days' the appropriate venue for a case (ie, Crown Court or magistrates' court) was decided before any plea was taken. If the magistrates' court thought that the case should be heard at the Crown Court, it would then be disqualified from hearing the defendant's plea. The case would then be sent to the Crown Court and the plea might not be taken for several months, since getting the case ready for the Crown Court is quite a lengthy process.

The system was changed so that the court could have an idea of what the plea was going to be *before* looking at the appropriate venue. The advantage of knowing the plea first lies in cases that are going to be sent up to the Crown Court. If the defendant wants to plead guilty, then the case can be sent to the Crown Court quickly, since no further investigation work would be required. If the defendant pleads not guilty then the officers carry on preparing the trial.

The only awkwardness about the system comes from the hugely long and drawn out explanations that the clerk/legal adviser offers to the defendant to explain what is going on. The court is keen to point out that in taking a plea at the magistrates' court there is no guarantee that the case will be disposed of at the magistrates' court. Explaining this is rather heavy going. For all the permutations of process, please see Appendix 2.

Procedure on a plea before venue

1 The clerk/legal adviser will ask something along the lines of 'are we ready for plea before venue?'.

2 If the Defence is ready to enter a plea, the advocate answers 'yes'. The clerk/legal adviser will then begin the process.

3 The court explains that it will take an indication of the defendant's plea and then decide which court will take the case thereafter.

4 The defendant is asked to indicate whether they understand.

5 The defendant is then asked to indicate if they will plead guilty or not guilty.

6 The defendant 'indicates' a plea. They say 'guilty' or 'not guilty' or they decline to indicate a plea at all (in which case the court will consider where to hear the case without knowing what the defendant intends to do). Not indicating a plea is very rare. An 'indication' of guilty or not guilty is sufficient for the court record and is counted as a proper plea in the case.

7 The prosecutor will outline facts to determine *either* where the *trial* should be heard (if there was either a not guilty indication or no indication) or where the *sentence* should be decided if the plea is guilty.

8 The Defence has the opportunity to address the court on the appropriate forum for trial or sentence. It may not be necessary or appropriate to make any comment if the decision on venue is obvious.

9 The bench then decides the appropriate venue for trial or sentence.

10 If the bench has offered summary trial after a not guilty indication then the defendant is asked whether they wish to elect Crown Court trial if the case is either way.

11 The court might proceed to sentence if the plea is guilty and suitable for summary disposal. Otherwise the case will be adjourned for whatever needs to be done next (sentence, trial or committal to the Crown Court).

What criteria does the court use to determine where a case should be heard?

Magistrates are issued with a publication called the *National Mode of Trial Guidelines*. Parts of this are copied out in *Blackstone's* which will assist a defence advocate to understand the decision that the magistrates are likely to come to in relation to venue.

Under s 19(3) of the Magistrates' Courts Act 1980, the magistrates should have regard to the following when considering where the case should be tried:

- The nature of the case.

- Whether the circumstances make the offence one of a serious character.

- Whether the magistrates' powers of sentencing are adequate.

- Any other circumstances which make the offence more suitable for one court than another.

Of all of the above, the usual starting point for examining where a case should be heard is whether the magistrates have sufficient powers of sentence. Magistrates can impose a maximum of six months' imprisonment for an offence and an aggregate of one year for two or more either way offences, and a fine of £5,000 for each offence. If a defendant has been charged with several offences, the magistrates should consider the offences together and not each one in isolation when deciding whether their sentencing powers are adequate.

The *National Mode of Trial Guidelines* (endorsed by the Lord Chief Justice and reissued in 1995) set out guidelines for deciding mode of trial, expanding on s 19(3) of the 1980 Act. Advocates should refer to these guidelines, which set out the features that should be taken into account regarding specific offences. The guidelines also make the following general observations:

- The court should not make its decision on the grounds of convenience or expedition.

- The court should assume that the Prosecution's version of the facts is correct.

- The fact that the offences are alleged to be specimens is relevant.

- The fact that the defendant will be asking for other offences to be taken into account if convicted is not relevant in determining the venue for a case.

- Where there are complex questions of law or fact the court should consider sending the case up to the Crown Court.

- Where there are two or more defendants, each has an individual right to elect their mode of trial.

- Generally, cases *should* be tried summarily unless the particular case has one or more of the features set out in the guidelines and the court's sentencing powers are insufficient.

- The court should consider its powers to commit a defendant for sentence under s 38 of the Magistrates' Courts Act 1980, as amended by s 25 of the Criminal Justice Act 1991.

Having made these general observations, the guidelines go on to analyse specific offences and mark up features of the offence that make any particular case more or less serious. For example, under the guidelines, features to look out for in theft or fraud cases are:

- Breach of trust by a person in a position of substantial authority, or in whom a high degree of trust is placed.

- Offence has been committed or disguised in a sophisticated manner.

- Offence has been committed by an organised gang.

- Victim is particularly vulnerable (eg, elderly).

- The unrecovered property is of high value (at least £10,000).

By looking at the guidelines, the defence advocate should gain some idea of how the magistrates are going to view the seriousness of the case. The crucial question will be whether the case as a whole (because there may be more than one charge) is so serious that the appropriate penalty on conviction is beyond the penalties available to the magistrates.

When should you advise a defendant to elect Crown Court trial?

The general rule is that the Crown Courts are better for trial (ie, more likely to acquit) but worse for sentence (ie, longer sentences).

There has been a lot of political discussion about the right to elect Crown Court trial. Some judges believe in this right absolutely, but others feel infuriated that vast sums of public money are spent on very simple and minor cases. If a defendant spends a day at trial putting forward a useless defence before a Crown Court judge who does not believe that the defendant should have the right to be there in the first place, the defendant can expect a significantly more serious sentence than if the defendant had stayed in the magistrates' court. The general rule should therefore extend to say that a defendant should be very wary of taking a trivial case with a poor defence to the Crown Court.

Consideration should be given to your geographical location, since this will influence the type of jury that may be assigned to hear the Crown Court trial. If you are dealing with offences of drugs, and the Crown Court is in a modern city, the chances are that the jury would be quite streetwise and modern in terms of attitudes to drugs. This might compare favourably with a bench of magistrates who are often older and more conservative than many juries. Juries in East London have a reputation for disbelieving police officers and acquitting at higher rates than in other parts of the country.

It may be that your local Crown Court is smaller, you know the reputation of the presiding judge and you can advise the client of what sort of sentence they might be facing if the case ends up being sentenced by judge X or Y.

The following are some factors that might help you decide on venue if the defendant has the right to elect.

Advantages of summary trial over jury trial

- Summary trial is generally much shorter.
- Summary trials tend to get heard much more quickly.
- A summary trial will be given a fixed date. (Note: most jury trials will be in a 'warned list', ie, the defendant is

only warned of a time frame within which the case may be listed.) Some jury cases are warned several times before they are actually finally heard. The anxiety of the wait for the defendant can be considerable.

- Summary trial will be less intimidating.

- The magistrates' powers of sentencing are far less than those of a Crown Court judge (although a defendant can in some circumstances be sent up to the Crown Court for sentence following summary trial).

- Summary trial is much cheaper if the defendant is not publicly funded.

Advantages of jury trial over summary trial

- A jury might be more sympathetic than magistrates and more likely to believe implausible stories.

- A jury might be less likely to believe police witnesses.

- There is a greater chance of acquittal as at least 10 people (rather than three magistrates) have to agree that the defendant is guilty.

- It is a more appropriate forum for extensive legal argument. If the case involves any application to exclude evidence the Crown Court has the advantage that the tribunal of fact and law are different. In the magistrates' court the bench will hear the disputed evidence and even if they rule it inadmissible the chances are that it will leave some impression upon them.

- You will be able to discuss aspects of the case (eg, admissibility of evidence) with your opponent more easily. Each Crown Court case is handled individually by a barrister and is not simply part of a long list. The attention to the case by the Prosecution is likely to increase at the Crown Court.

- You may agree a plea bargain that was not accepted by the Crown Prosecution Service (CPS) representative at the magistrates' court. The Defence often finds that it is hard to strike a deal in the magistrates' court since the CPS uses agents to prosecute on its behalf who are not authorised to accept alternative or part pleas. Once the case gets to the Crown Court it will be reviewed by the barrister instructed by the Prosecution who may take a more even-handed approach than the CPS caseworker.

Making representations about venue

The main occasion on which defence advocates will want to make a representation about the appropriate venue is after a guilty plea, where the bench is considering whether to commit the defendant to the Crown Court for sentence.

Clearly the Crown Court has wider powers, and the Defence may seek to 'cap' the sentence by encouraging the magistrates' court to keep jurisdiction. This is done by referring the bench to the main areas of mitigation available to the defendant and encouraging the bench to accept that the case is not sufficiently serious to exceed the magistrates' powers.

It is not always right to suppose that a defendant will be treated more severely in the Crown Court. In many cases Crown Court judges are less inclined to pass custodial sentences than lay magistrates. For example, Crown Court judges have much broader experience of persistent offenders who have only become worse criminals since being sent to custody. Many judges are more cynical of the effectiveness of custody as a punishment than are magistrates, and some judges are quite prepared to take a gamble in trying to effect a defendant's rehabilitation in the community.

In addition, it seems to be the case that many Crown Court judges view offences involving Class B drugs less seriously than lay magistrates do. The reason being that Crown Court judges see much worse crime caused through drink and class A drugs and therefore Class B drugs seem a less pressing priority. Some benches, with less criminal experience, may take a harder view of the effect of Class B drugs on society.

There is much generalisation and little science when it comes to deciding where it would be best for a defendant to be sentenced. Advocates simply have to think hard about the case at hand and decide (if the case is borderline) whether there is really any obvious advantage in trying to persuade a bench to accept or decline jurisdiction.

For trial, it is better to be committed than to elect

This is a small but important point. If the defendant is pleading not guilty and wants a Crown Court trial, it is better for them if the magistrates commit to the Crown Court than if they elect. If the defendant elects trial and loses, the judge may take the view that *the defendant* has wasted public time and money by electing to have the case heard in the Crown Court which is much more expensive. However, *if the magistrates committed* the case for trial, no blame can attach to the defendant at all. To put the point of cost to the taxpayer in context, the average cost of a Crown Court case is said to be £8,600, compared with £550 in the magistrates' court (Home Office research, 1999). The Defence should try to avoid having a Crown Court judge punishing the defendant for exercising their right to elect trial if at all possible.

Consequently it would actually be very good practice for defence advocates to try to persuade the Prosecution and the court that they should commit the trial to the Crown Court rather than leaving it to the defendant to elect the Crown Court. It would be unusual to invite the court openly to commit a case, but you can be subtler and say something along the lines of:

> I accept that there are some features of this case that make it serious, and I would not seek to persuade you to offer jurisdiction.

Prosecutors

The CPS file should say whether the prosecution advocate is to submit that the case is either suitable for summary trial or not suitable for summary trial. This is often noted on the front cover of the file and abbreviated to SST (suitable for summary trial) or NSST (not suitable for summary trial). Prosecutors should endorse the file with what was represented by the Prosecution and by the Defence and record the court's decision. The prosecutor should then note whether the defendant elects trial.

Whilst prosecutors should make representations about venue when a defendant indicates a not guilty plea, it is *inappropriate* to pass comment on the appropriate venue for *sentence*. This is because sentence is a matter between the court and the Defence. The Prosecution does no more than to put the facts to the court to aid the court in determining sentence. Unlike America, the Prosecution should not attempt to persuade or influence the court into passing any particular form of sentence and this extends to attempting to persuade the court about the appropriate *forum* for sentence. The Prosecution is asked to relay the facts and there is no prohibition in explaining the facts forcefully. All that must be avoided is direct comment on where a sentencing hearing should be heard or what the sentence should be.

10   Entering a plea

If the Defence has received advance disclosure and has had enough time to consider it, the Defence must then give advice and take instructions on how the defendant wishes to plead. Some defendants will have made up their minds and nothing their advocate will say will make any difference; others will be undecided and will ask for assistance.

Terminology

People tend to use the expression 'pleading' to mean 'pleading guilty'.

Pleading not guilty and going to trial could be described as:

- going to trial;
- fighting a case;
- contesting a case;
- having 'a runner'.

Advising the defendant: guilty or not guilty?

First and foremost, advocates have a duty to advise their client as to whether they have a defence in law. Having taken instructions on what the defendant said took place, the advocate will then be able to say whether there is a defence in law.

The most common defence is, 'I did not do it' but the position is often much more difficult than that. 'Provocation' as a defence is a common problem area of advising, since it is *no defence* (except to murder). Another common problem area for advising comes with the awkwardly worded public order offences. Watch out too for possession of an offensive weapon and possession of a bladed article where different defences are available according to which offence is charged. The point is that the advocate must be absolutely clear about what is or is not a defence to the charge and no advice should be attempted unless or until the necessary research has been done.

Having identified whether there is a defence even available, the advocate will need to advise on the merits of the defence being successful. The reason for giving this advice is to probe and make sure that the defendant is going to enter the correct plea.

Advising the defendant to plead guilty (because the evidence is strong)

Some defendants seem very confident, even aggressive, about being not guilty. This often masks all sorts of anxieties, so be careful not to take this at face value. If the evidence against the defendant is strong, and a conviction is highly likely, an advocate does need to explore this and test their instructions carefully.

The scenario that advocates must avoid is failing to advise adequately on the consequences of going to trial and being convicted. Any sentence in any case will depend in part upon whether the defendant pleaded guilty or was convicted after trial. If a conviction appears to be inevitable and the advocate fails to advise about the benefits of pleading guilty, the advocate has failed their professional duty to advise.

The consequences of this failure can really become apparent when the bench turns to sentence where it may well remark that the sentence being passed would have been different if the defendant had pleaded guilty. A plea of guilty can sometimes be the difference between a custodial sentence and a non-custodial sentence. If the defendant has not appreciated the serious consequences of contesting a case and losing, this is a serious breach of duty to advise.

Consequently, you need to be very careful to advise both on the merits of the case, and on what going to trial might mean if you lose the case. This is especially important where a conviction is likely.

It is normal to hear *advocates* saying that they 'advised the defendant to plead guilty', but it is not advisable to use the phrase 'I advise you to plead guilty' to the defendant. If you say 'I advise you to plead guilty' it can be hard to retain the trust and confidence of the defendant if the defendant instructs the advocate that he wants to plead not guilty.

Every advocate has a different way of broaching the issue of plea with a client, and there is no formula for doing so. The advocate is duty bound to advise a client on the merits of their case, and this needs to be undertaken carefully, and without annoying the defendant. You might want to approach it along the following lines:

> You have the right to know my professional view of what is likely to happen in your case. I think that there are some difficulties on the facts. They are [explanation of weaknesses in the case]. So my conclusion is that you are likely to be convicted.

> If you say that you are not guilty, then that is the end of the matter, and I will defend you to the best of my ability.

> I am duty bound to advise you of the credit which is on offer to those who plead guilty, and, given the weaknesses of your case, I would advise you to consider carefully if you really are not guilty, because you should seriously consider taking advantage of the offer of credit for pleading guilty if you are guilty.

When you give advice, you are only advising on what *a court* might think or do. You are not passing any form of personal judgment on the defendant or the case. Sometimes it is worth reminding the defendant of this and indicating that you are only predicting the court and discussing the defendant's options. You are not giving a personal view (and you will not do so, even if asked) and you are obliged to give the defendant advice as to the options.

Pleading guilty for tactical reasons

It may be that the defendant has decided that they want to plead guilty for reasons other than actually being guilty. The most usual of these is in order to 'get it over with' as soon as possible.

Defendants are permitted to plead guilty even when they say that they are not guilty – but it is unusual and undesirable. The issue to be aware of is that you would be barred from 'going behind the plea'. This means that you cannot mitigate on the basis that this defendant has not committed the offence. The court has to proceed on the basis that the defendant is guilty, so saying that they actually are not guilty is not a worthwhile exercise.

This leaves you with very little to say, and the defendant would be better off pleading guilty for the conventional reason (that they are guilty) and letting you do your job of mitigating. Once you explain this to a client, 99 times out of 100 they will concede that they are guilty. Defendants sometimes think that if they say they will plead 'just to get it over with' then they can argue their innocence in mitigation. The advocate should advise that the court can take no notice of any mitigation which seeks to deny guilt. Once they are told this, the advocate will usually find that clients will plead guilty and admit that they are guilty.

Pleading not guilty for tactical reasons

There are a few occasions when you might find that you are putting in a not guilty plea when the defendant is guilty and knows it.

- *Witness attendance*

A defendant might wish to avoid pleading guilty where there is a question about whether a witness will attend court or not on the day of trial. In domestic violence cases one sees this time after time. One partner is charged with violence against the other. The evidence is strong, but reliant upon one party in the relationship giving evidence against the other. By the time the case comes to trial, the relationship is improved, the parties are reconciled, and the original complainant does not want to come to court to give evidence. The Prosecution can send round a police car and bring the witness in, but, often, if the witness is really unwilling to give evidence and retracts the allegation, then the Prosecution is likely to have to discontinue the case.

The defendant will lose the credit of an early guilty plea if they hold out to see if the witness actually makes it to court and the witness does do so. The defendant may feel that it is worth the risk!

• *Special events*

Another reason for delaying a guilty plea includes the desire to be on bail for special events. It is understandable that many defendants plead not guilty and are on bail *before* Christmas and have a change of heart and plead guilty and accept a custodial sentence *after* Christmas. The same goes for events such as the birth of children.

So if the defendant is likely to get a custodial sentence but would probably get bail, and is desperate to be 'on the outside' for a particular reason, you may well find that a not guilty plea (and bail) will be followed by a guilty plea (and custody) later on. Any defence advocate *must* make sure that the defendant understands that they will lose credit for not pleading guilty at the first opportunity.

Credit for plea – how much?

It is always important to consider and to advise on the level of credit that is available and might be given in any particular case.

The general rule is that a plea at the first opportunity attracts one-third off any sentence. Credit for a plea can actually influence the type of sentence, and mitigate a case down from a short custodial sentence to a non-custodial sentence.

There are factors that influence and adjust the amount of credit:

• *The strength of the evidence*

A defendant who was caught red-handed may receive less credit since, really, there is little credit to attach to someone who has no realistic option but to plead guilty. On the other hand, in the case of someone who pleads guilty when there is an arguable defence available (eg, self-defence) or where they might have been able to rely on a procedural or evidential argument at trial, then it is particularly creditable that they did *not* run the defence, but accepted guilt.

- *The nature of the case*

Some cases are difficult and sensitive and having the trial would cause some particular hardship to a particular person. There may be a scared or vulnerable witness involved, or the need for expensive experts or lengthy argument on some moot point. A defendant might get special credit for averting difficult trials, but the better way to view this is that if the defendant were *not* to avert the difficult trial, then there would be special and additional *aggravating* features on sentence. Defence advocates need to look at the nature of the case and try to envisage how the trial would influence the court's view of the defendant. If the advocate takes the view that the trial would make the court view the defendant in a particularly bad light, then the defendant should be properly advised of the merits of pleading guilty.

Plea bargaining and Newton hearings

- *Plea bargaining*

Accepting a plea bargain is in essence a deal between the Prosecution and Defence, involving the Prosecution offering no evidence in respect of certain charges in return for a guilty plea in respect of others. It also applies to the Defence offering and the Prosecution accepting a guilty plea to a lesser offence than the one with which the defendant was charged.

If the elements of an offence include, either expressly or impliedly, another offence, the defendant could be found guilty of that 'included' offence, even if it is not formally charged. Examples include theft when charged with burglary or robbery, common assault when charged with causing actual bodily harm, indecent assault when charged with rape, actual bodily harm or theft when charged with robbery, s 20 of the Offences Against the Person Act 1861 (unlawful wounding) when charged with s 18 (wounding with intent) and careless driving when charged with dangerous driving.

The advantage to the defendant of a plea bargain is that the sentence will be less than if it were based on the original offence charged. If a defendant is contemplating running a defence that is unlikely to succeed, they will probably prefer to plead guilty to something more minor or to some but not all of the charges and to avoid going through a trial which may end in conviction. If you feel that there is scope for a plea bargain you should discuss the implications with the defendant, but do not advise the defendant to enter a guilty plea if they insist that they have not committed the offence to which you suggest pleading.

Defence advocates need to be aware of the practical difficulties of plea bargaining in the magistrates' court. If the prosecutor is an agent for the Crown Prosecution Service, or if the prosecutor is in the CPS but junior, it may be that they lack the authority to bargain over plea, and the case would have to be adjourned, 'for the defence to make representations' which is the usual shorthand for plea bargaining. You may find that your prosecutor is able and willing to make a deal, but do not assume this.

• *Pleading on a 'basis'*

The other option available is to plead guilty on a particular basis. For example, the Prosecution might say that the defendant is guilty of an assault, which is made up of two punches and three kicks. The defendant accepts one punch and no kicks at all. This is tricky – you both accept that they are guilty of an offence, but you have a different idea of what the offence actually is.

The first thing to do is to ask the prosecutor if they would accept your more limited version of the facts. If the answer is 'yes', you are then going to have to rely on the prosecutor giving your version of the incident to the court that is going to pass sentence. If the sentence is going to go ahead on the same day as the plea, you will have the same prosecutor who agreed the deal with you. If there is an adjournment for a pre-sentence report, the Defence has the problem of making sure that the person who comes to prosecute the case in the future honours the 'deal'.

The only really safe thing to do is to put the deal *in writing*. So what the Defence does in practice is to write down the basis of the plea, eg, 'the defendant pleads guilty on the basis that there was a *single blow*' and the Defence gets the prosecutor to sign this.

When the case returns to court, if you are defending, you need to confirm that the prosecutor on the day is aware that the Prosecution has formally accepted that the offence is now to be described in the agreed and more limited way.

Whether the Prosecution accepts the Defence's version of the facts will depend upon its confidence in proving the remainder of its case. To use the example of the assault, it may be that the victim was being attacked by a number of people, and although there is *some* evidence that this particular defendant was responsible for three punches, it is not impossible that the victim is wrong about who did what, and perhaps the defendant is actually right. Therefore, in order to persuade the Prosecution to accept your limited version of events, you need to persuade the Prosecution that it would be hard to prove any more than you are offering.

The fact that the Prosecution and Defence have agreed the facts between them is not the end of the story. The magistrates or District Judge are entitled to investigate the background of an offence so that the court is sure of how to sentence. It is possible, therefore, for the court to demand that the Prosecution put the witness before the court to explore the facts of the case.

This is rare in the magistrates' court. It is more common in the Crown Court, mainly because the Crown Court judges will have read the papers beforehand and will have formed their own professional view of what is capable of being proved or not.

If you make an offer to the Prosecution of pleading guilty on a more limited basis, and the Prosecution is *not* willing to accept this version of events, then the Prosecution would ask the court to hear evidence. This is not a trial of guilt, since guilt of an offence has already been accepted. The hearing is to ascertain the facts that will form the basis of sentence. The subsequent hearing is called a 'Newton' hearing – named after the case where this procedure was first properly recognised and adopted.

Ultimately, it is up to the magistrates to decide whether it is necessary to hear any evidence. If the Prosecution's case is that there was an assault involving three punches and two kicks, and the defendant instructs that it was three punches and one kick, it would not seem to make much difference to sentence either way. The Defence would say that the Prosecution should not bother trying to prove the extra kick – it would make no difference to sentence either way. The Prosecution's view on whether there should be a hearing to prove the extra kick will certainly influence the court strongly, but the final decision on whether to put the dispute to a hearing rests with the magistrates.

Summary of the procedure for dealing on the basis of plea

- The defendant pleads guilty.
- The defence advocate makes it plain that the plea is offered on a limited basis.
- The Prosecution then indicates whether the basis is acceptable so far as it is concerned.
- If the Prosecution says the basis is unacceptable so far as the Prosecution is concerned, the Defence still has the right to ask the court to conclude that there is no merit in hearing any evidence to resolve the matter and to sentence the case on the defendant's version.

- The court decides whether or not to hear any evidence. The court should not call evidence if it does not matter for sentence which way the offence was committed. It should have evidence called if there is a genuine and substantial difference in accounts of the offence from the Prosecution and the Defence.

If the court wishes to hear evidence about how the offence was committed, the case will have to be adjourned, either directly to a date on which evidence will be called, or to an interim date to allow the Prosecution to contact the witnesses and check their availability to attend court.

Prosecutors

There is little to add for prosecutors in terms of plea. The advice that is repeated throughout this book is that any advocate instructed as an agent for the Crown Prosecution Service (CPS) must be very careful about making decisions on how to proceed with a case. Decisions about the conduct of a case should be referred to the CPS lawyer concerned.

If the Defence offers to plead guilty to a reasonable proportion of the offences charged, or offers to plead guilty on a reasonable basis, the best course of action is to attempt to contact the lawyer in the case. Be prepared to remind the lawyer about the case. It is very important to seek authorisation to accept the plea. The court would not be able to proceed with a case without knowing whether the Prosecution accepted the Defence pleas (or their basis) and the only real alternative to the Prosecution stating its view is to adjourn the case. A few years ago, courts would routinely adjourn cases for the CPS to consider any representations from the Defence about pleas, but there is considerable pressure now for the courts to make progress and the courts generally prefer to give the prosecutor a moment to make a telephone call to the CPS rather than to adjourn the case.

The Defence routinely suggests a plea bargain (or a basis of plea) on the morning of the trial. If this is the case, then it is important to secure the view of the officer in the case (assuming that he or she is at court as a witness) and even the view of the 'victim' in the case before consulting the CPS lawyer. The CPS does not generally approve of accepting partial pleas on the morning of the trial unless there is some support for this course of action from the police and the main witness(es).

What if ...?

- *The defendant admits the offence but wants to plead not guilty?*

If the defendant actually admits that they have committed the offence, you must advise (but not compel) them to plead guilty. If the defendant maintains that they do not wish to plead guilty, you can only put the Prosecution's witnesses 'to proof' when cross-examining. This means that you simply check whether they have given evidence of an offence being committed. You cannot assert a case contrary to the Prosecution's case; you can only seek to discredit it.

For example, if the witness says that they saw a man who fitted the defendant's description commit an act, you can ask about the lighting, and ask if the witness is sure, but you cannot suggest that they are wrong. 99 times out of 100, putting the Crown to proof is a hopeless exercise. You are really impotent in making any attack on the prosecution case.

You can make a submission of no case at the close of the prosecution case but, if unsuccessful, you cannot call the defendant to give evidence. This is because you know that they are guilty and that they propose to lie in their evidence. If you knowingly allowed the defendant to lie to the court, you would be acting against the code of conduct.

If the defendant tells you one thing and then contradicts their instructions to you, you should tell the court that you are unable to represent the defendant because you are professionally embarrassed. You do *not* need to explain why and tell everyone in open court that the defendant is a liar! You may want to ask for an adjournment so that the defendant can instruct someone else. If you are a solicitor, tell the defendant that they will have to go to a different firm; if you are counsel, tell your instructing solicitor that you are professionally embarrassed and it is up to them whether they feel that they can continue to represent the defendant with different counsel.

- *The defendant wishes to change the plea already entered?*

From not guilty to guilty
This can be done at any stage prior to the decision to convict or acquit. When the next hearing is the trial, the Defence should contact the Prosecution to inform them of the change of plea in order that the witnesses can be de-warned. In any case, the court should be informed that the time set aside will no longer be required so that the case can be re-listed for a plea if necessary. The advocate should try to obtain the defendant's written confirmation that they intend to plead guilty.

From guilty to not guilty
The court has discretion to allow a defendant to change a plea from guilty to not guilty at any time prior to sentence. However, this discretion will be used sparingly and only in clear cases when the plea was entered by genuine mistake. Where a defendant has been represented throughout the proceedings, it will be difficult to persuade the magistrates or District Judge to exercise their discretion in the defendant's favour, since it would appear that the defendant received adequate advice throughout.

The usual reason that a defendant gives for having entered a guilty plea, and then asking to enter a not guilty plea, is that the plea of guilty was forced upon them. The defendant will say that their representative gave them 'no choice' but to plead guilty. It is unattractive to have to argue in court that the defendant's previous representative effectively forced the defendant to plead guilty against their will.

Many lawyers adopt the practice of 'endorsing the brief'. This means that before a defendant pleads guilty, the lawyer acting for them will make them sign a declaration that the plea of guilty is made of their own free will, and that they plead guilty because they are guilty. If there is such an endorsement, then it will be next to impossible for the defendant to change the plea back again.

11   Committal proceedings

The committal is the process of passing the case from the magistrates' court to the Crown Court. If a defendant has indicated a guilty plea and the court has decided to commit the case to the Crown Court for sentence, there is no committal hearing – the case is simply sent to the Crown Court with no more ado. If the defendant pleaded not guilty, then the case will be listed one more time in the magistrates' court.

There are two types of committal. In short, there are contested committals and non-contested committals. The magistrates' court has a power to refuse to commit a case to the Crown Court if the magistrates' court takes the view that there is no case for the Defence to answer. The Prosecution meets its first deadline at committal and must have produced some basic case against the defendant. If there is some evidence in the case, then the Defence should not contest the committal and the hearing is very short and effectively administrative. Both types of hearings are described in more detail below.

Terminology

A committal where the Defence wishes to challenge the committal is called by a number of names including:

- a contested committal;
- a 6(1) committal;
- a read-through committal;
- an 'old style' committal;
- a committal with consideration of the evidence.

The reasons for these names will become clear when this form of committal is discussed below.

An uncontested committal is normally called a 'paper committal' or more normally a 6(2) committal.

What is the purpose of contesting a committal?

The Magistrates' Courts Act (MCA) 1980 gives the magistrates' court the power to examine a case and to decline to commit the case to the Crown Court if there appears to be insufficient evidence to put before a jury. It is basically a screening process so that cases that are somehow defective are not sent to the Crown Court. The power is conferred in s 6(1), hence the name a '6(1) committal'.

Section 6(1) is drafted narrowly, in that the Prosecution only has to show that it has evidence of *any* indictable offence. This is very significant in practice. Say, for example, that the defendant is charged with four offences of burglary. At the time of committal, the Prosecution has not served evidence to support more than one of the burglaries. On the other charges, there is either no evidence of burglary, or evidence only of handling. None of these defects would concern the Prosecution at this stage, since the committal can be limited to the one case of burglary for which there is some evidence, with the other charges being added at the Crown Court (so long as they are part of a series). Contesting a committal is, therefore, only really worthwhile if the defendant is charged with a single offence, or where the Defence can submit that there is no evidence of *any indictable offence*.

If the committal is successfully contested the defendant is discharged. This does not amount to an acquittal and so it is possible that the defendant could be arrested again and the proceedings started over again. The Prosecution may take the view that it would not be in the public interest to attempt to bring proceedings a second time, and the delay in getting the case to trial would be likely to be long and potentially subject to an argument of abuse of process. It is important to remind a defendant that a discharge at committal does not guarantee the conclusion of any proceedings.

The test used to determine whether to commit

The MCA 1980 test is a vague one. It states simply that the court should only commit a case if there 'is sufficient evidence to put before a jury'. The courts have chosen to read this test as if it were the same as the test for a submission of no case to answer. This is the submission that is available to the Defence at trial, where, on hearing the prosecution case it appears that there is no evidence on which any reasonable tribunal could safely convict. This is helpful to an extent but not absolutely so, since in a trial the Defence has the opportunity to discredit evidence by cross-examination. There is no cross-examination in a committal, and the application to have the case dismissed is simply on the basis of a reading of the papers.

Whilst there is no definitive statement of the test involved, the idea is that the magistrates should not commit a case that has no realistic prospects of being prosecuted to a conviction. If there is any credible chance that the Prosecution might succeed in gaining a conviction on the basis of the evidence at committal, then the case should be committed.

The form of the hearing at a contested committal

There was a time when the committal would run much like a trial, and the Prosecution would call live evidence and there would be cross-examination. Nowadays, there is still consideration of the evidence in a contested committal, but the examination of the prosecution case is entirely *on the papers.*

The Prosecution will normally make an opening statement, setting out the background to the offence and indicating the nature of the evidence that will be submitted to support the committal. The prosecutor will then read the statements out. The Prosecution and Defence should talk before the hearing, and agree, where possible, where the evidence can simply be summarised. It may be possible to summarise the whole case and proceed directly to submissions. The procedure is flexible to allow the case to be dealt with as efficiently as possible.

There is a provision for the Prosecution to call a witness and take a deposition from the witness as a part of the trial process. This is rarely used.

Once the prosecutor has read the statements out and/or summarised other parts of the statements so that the prosecution case is complete, the Defence would then make the application to dismiss the case. The Defence may not call any evidence nor refer to what evidence the Defence would propose to give at trial. This is an examination of the prosecution case. The submission is based entirely on whether the Prosecution has raised enough evidence for the court to suppose that the defendant should be asked to stand trial.

The Prosecution has the right to reply to the submission.

The court will then consider whether to commit to the Crown Court, or to dismiss the defendant. When deliberating, the court is entitled to view exhibits and re-read any of the statements.

Editing statements and arguing admissibility

The committal is *not usually* the right forum to argue for dismissal of the case on the basis that the prosecution case is based on inadmissible evidence. Ruling evidence admissible or otherwise is a matter for the trial judge. It is not generally appropriate for a magistrates' court to rule that evidence is inadmissible when the Crown Court trial judge may take the contrary view. The courts have not *barred* the magistrates' court from ruling evidence as inadmissible, but the magistrates are urged only to rule evidence as inadmissible in the most extreme and obvious cases.

Although the court is unlikely to rule that evidence is inadmissible for the reasons just set out, it is possible that the Prosecution may agree to edit the evidence complained of. Statements are often edited to strike out passages thought to be inadmissible. Editing at trial is normally done by blotting out the passage concerned so that the court cannot see what was previously written. This is *not* the right procedure for committal. At committal, the Prosecution should draw brackets around the inadmissible evidence and the index of the statements should include an indication that the Prosecution is not seeking to rely on those statements struck out, or the parts of those statements that are bracketed.

An uncontested committal

Uncontested committals are short and largely administrative hearings. The Prosecution will serve a 'committal bundle' on the Defence at court if this has not already been done. The committal bundle is effectively the Crown Court brief, with the typed witness statements for the prosecution witnesses and a draft indictment.

The advocate should take receipt of the bundle and then answer several questions from the clerk/legal adviser. These questions are:

- 'Are you intending to make any submission to have the case dismissed?' This is basically to check that this is an uncontested committal and not a contested one! For what to do if the court is expecting an uncontested committal and the Defence wants to contest the committal, see 'What if ...?' section below.

- 'Are there any applications relating to publicity restrictions?' There is a general rule that the details of a case should not be reported so that a potential jury is not influenced by the publicity about them. The Defence can apply for these to be lifted. If such application is made, it must be granted. If there are two defendants and one wishes the restriction to be lifted, and the other does not, the court will only lift the restrictions 'in the interests of justice'. Applications to lift publicity restrictions are rare and generally confined to cases where the defendant may need publicity (for example, to encourage witnesses to come forward on their behalf) or simply desires publicity for some wider reason (for example, for a political reason).

The other matters raised will be:

- The right to object to statements being read. The Prosecution will read the statements of the witnesses unless the Defence objects to their being read. Such objections should be made on a form that is handed out at the committal. There is no need to fill it in there and then; there is a 14-day period to lodge the form. The issue of which witness statements should be read and which witnesses called will be revisited at the plea and directions hearing in the Crown Court in any event.

- Representation order. The court has the power to extend representation to the Crown Court, subject to the defendant being means tested under Form B. The Defence should ask for representation to be extended to the Crown Court orally at the committal hearing, and the Defence should take Form B for completion that day or soon thereafter. The extension of representation is effectively automatic and the advocate usually need not prepare any application of substance. There might be a review of the appropriateness of representation in a case where the charges have been reduced to almost insignificant levels and where the defendant has elected Crown Court trial when magistrates' court trial would have seemed appropriate. In these circumstances it may be as well to prepare to argue the merits of having representation, otherwise the court will not trouble the Defence for its reasons in any detail.

- Bail. It is rare to alter the status quo at committal. If the defendant is in custody, the fact that the case has now reached committal and will be sent to the Crown Court is not a 'change in circumstances' permitting a new bail application. However, if the committal bundle discloses some change in the way that the Prosecution puts the case, then there may be a change of circumstances.

Prosecutors

In addition to the above, the clerk/legal adviser will ask the prosecutor to hand into the court all the original handwritten statements. These should be somewhere in the file.

What if ...?

- *The court has listed the case as an uncontested committal, and the Defence wants to contest the committal?*

The court needs to put time aside for a contested committal. If the Defence has not notified the court of its request for a contested committal, it is unlikely that the court would have the time to hear the contested hearing and an adjournment would be required.

It is the duty of the Defence to notify the court that it wishes to contest the committal. If the Defence has simply failed to do so then the court is likely to criticise the Defence for wasting time. Since the delay is to the defendant's prejudice then the court is unlikely to do any more than complain about the Defence being disorganised. It is unlikely that there will be any issue of costs since the only wasted hearing would be the redundant uncontested committal, which is only a five-minute hearing anyway.

Whilst there may simply have been an error in not notifying the court of the Defence's request for a contested hearing, the more likely scenario is that the advocate taking the brief for the committal takes the view that there should be a contested committal where the lawyer(s) previously dealing with the case had not thought to request such a hearing. If this is the situation in which you find yourself, you will need to speak to the person primarily dealing with the case and discuss whether they share your view that a contested committal would be a worthwhile exercise. The lawyer may be unavailable, and you may need to make the decision yourself. Ultimately, it is for the defendant to instruct you to make the application but, as this is a technical area, the reality is that they will instruct you to do what you advise. Be careful to advise on the delay to having the trial that would be incurred by adjourning the case to arrange a contested committal.

If the defence advocate holding the brief/file on the day genuinely believes that the defendant's interests would be best served by applying to adjourn the case to find time to hear a contested committal, then this is the course that should be adopted. Before seeking such an adjournment, be realistic about what might be achieved. It is difficult to have a case dismissed at the committal stage.

- *The court is expecting a contested committal, and the Defence decides against contesting the committal?*

It may be that one defence advocate considers that there would be merit in contesting the committal, and then passes the case to another advocate who sees no merit in this course of action at all. There is nothing to prevent the Defence simply changing its mind on the day of committal as to the form of committal. The court is likely to be frustrated as the court is thereby left empty and unproductive but further than that the defendant is entitled to accept the committal having earlier indicating that there would be a contest.

If court time has been given to the hearing and the defendant is expecting a contested committal, it would be worth going through with the exercise even if the defence advocate on the day is more sceptical about the prospects of success than the lawyer who asked for the hearing.

If the Prosecution serves more evidence on the day of committal and thereby remedies the defect in the case, then it would be best to abandon the contested committal and proceed with the uncontested version.

12 Reviewing readiness for trial and pre-trial reviews

You will always need to keep an eye on any case to advance that case towards a state where it can be said that it is properly ready for trial. There are hearings sometimes called pre-trial reviews (PTR), and sometimes now called by the new name of criminal directions hearings (CDH). This chapter reviews what you need to be aware of throughout a case and what you should know about for the purposes of the PTR/CDH.

Check that you have all the evidence

Disclosure (getting all the information from the Crown) is so important that it is dealt with separately (see Chapter 13).

It is not only a question of getting documents from the Crown, but also ensuring that there are statements or proofs of evidence from the defendant and other potential defence witnesses. If, at any point in proceedings, the defendant gives you information which tends to suggest there may be unexplored evidence, make a firm note of this and tell the solicitor whose case it is what enquiries ought to be made.

Instructing an expert

It may be necessary to instruct an expert witness, eg, a medical expert or graphologist. When preparing the case, consider whether it is necessary to obtain expert evidence. If so, do so as soon as possible as experts tend to be very busy and take a long time to prepare their reports. It may strike you that an expert is required and nothing has yet been done about it. You should raise the matter as soon as possible with whoever's case it is. You will need to apply for public funding for the expert, or ask a privately paying client if they are prepared to pay for the expert. So far as public funding is concerned, you are unlikely to secure public funding if the expert is not critical to the case or if the case is too minor to warrant a major expense.

There are many experts and half the battle is even realising what experts can be called upon to say. Here are some ideas!

- Doctors are amongst the most commonly consulted experts and routinely give evidence on whether injuries caused are consistent with the explanations given by the various parties.

- The Prosecution sometimes adduces DNA and fingerprint expert evidence.

- There are experts who compare the way that drugs are wrapped and who can thus establish whether drugs found in place A came from the same source as drugs found in place B. The drug itself can also be chemically analysed to compare the purity and cutting agent of the two batches.

- There are experts who can lip-read from CCTV to interpret what someone is saying on CCTV.

- There are experts on how alcohol is absorbed into the body. They are used in drink-driving cases where the results of a breath test are contaminated by drinking after driving but before performing the test.

- There are experts who analyse the pattern of blood splattering to shed light on how a wound was caused.

- There are cell site experts who can look at the databases of mobile phone companies to see which cell site picked up a particular call. This helps to locate where a call was made from.

- There are scratch pattern experts who can comment on whether a given implement could have caused the damage observed to a particular lock.

- There are experts who can give opinions on how much cannabis might be cultivated from a particular method of cultivation.

- In forged document cases you may need a handwriting analyst.

Interviews

Interviews with a defendant at a police station are tape-recorded and the Defence is entitled to a copy of the recording. The Prosecution will also produce a transcript of the recording. This is often summarised in parts so it is worth listening to the recording to check the accuracy of the transcript and to find out what has been left out.

If the Defence wishes anything to be added to the transcript, it should seek the Prosecution's agreement or ask for the tape-recording to be played. If the Defence wishes anything to be omitted from the transcript, eg, reference to the defendant's previous convictions or any prejudicial hearsay, the Defence should ask the Prosecution to cross out the relevant passages in the transcript. This is often done on the morning of the trial but it ought to be done beforehand.

Admissibility of statements (or parts thereof)

If you are defending and if you have been served with advance information or a committal bundle, go through the prosecution witness statements looking out for inadmissible evidence, eg, hearsay. Make a note of any inadmissible evidence and notify the Crown Prosecution Service (CPS) that you object to it, either before the day of the trial or on the morning of the trial. Make sure that you tell the prosecutor which evidence you object to before the trial begins so that they do not open the evidence that is in dispute. Ask the prosecutor to agree that the evidence is excluded. If the prosecutor will not agree to exclude evidence that you think is inadmissible, you will have to challenge its admissibility. This is done by way of a trial within a trial or *voir dire*.

More often than not, issues of admissibility are not raised until the morning of the trial. Trials are regularly held up on account of such details not being dealt with earlier.

Considering an abuse of process argument

Abuse of process is, eg, where the Crown has lost exhibits, acted unfairly or taken so long with the proceedings that to proceed with the case at all becomes unreasonable. Abuse of process is a large topic and you will need to read *Archbold* (2002 London: Sweet & Maxwell) or *Blackstone's* (2003, Oxford: OUP). In short, you need to apply to the discretion of the court to stay (dismiss) proceedings because there has been genuine unfairness to the trial of the defendant through some action or inaction on behalf of the Prosecution.

There is no definitive list of what counts as abuse of process, and case law is said only to provide a guide. All cases turn on their own facts. For the power of a magistrates' court to stay proceedings, the leading case is *R v Horseferry Road Magistrates' Court ex p Bennett* [1994] 1 AC 42. The principle laid down is that the magistrates can stay the proceedings *only* where there are matters that directly affect the fairness of the trial of the accused.

The following represent the general consensus about abuse of process:

- An application that the proceedings constitute an abuse of process can be made at any stage pre-trial.

- A criminal court can stay the proceedings if it agrees.

- Abuse should be narrowly defined.

- You cannot claim abuse of process merely because you think that the Crown does not have much evidence against a defendant.

- There does not have to be bad faith to show abuse of process.

- There is often some complaint about the *process* of justice, and therefore most complaints are about delay in proceedings. This is not necessarily so in all cases.

- The abuse of process will usually be argued on the basis that a fair trial cannot proceed. But this is not *inevitably* the case. The power exists to stop the administration of justice coming into disrepute, and to stop the courts from being an instrument of oppression (cf *Re Barings plc and Others, etc* [1999] 1 All ER 311, CA).

• Any point that should be properly taken at trial should not be taken as a point of abuse of process. The trial process itself is equipped to deal with most complaints.

Nine times out of 10, abuse of process arguments relate to disclosure and the failure of the Crown to produce documents that it should have done. In the case of CCTV, the videotapes are often lost or recorded over before the police or CPS do anything to save the evidence.

One can make an abuse of process argument at any point in proceedings. If the Prosecution has the chance to rectify a problem quickly, an application for abuse will be unlikely to succeed. It may still be a good idea to make the application since the application may provoke the court into setting down an instruction (eg, that the Crown will disclose a document by date X) even when it actually grants the adjournment. You can always ask the court to indicate that if the direction is not complied with then the case should not be further adjourned. This indication is not binding on a future court but it does give you ammunition to have the case dismissed next time if the Prosecution has still failed to do as directed.

Considering severance

If you are defending one of a number of defendants, you should consider whether all the defendants should be tried together or separately. Hearing a case against more than one defendant is appropriate if the offences separately alleged against the defendants are so closely related, eg, by time, that the interests of justice are best served by a single trial. The court has a discretion to order separate trials, eg, where a joint trial against a large number of defendants would result in a very long trial. As a general rule, the court will usually order a joint trial unless the risk of prejudice is very great.

If you are defending a defendant charged with a number of offences, you should consider whether all the charges should be tried together. Charges for any offences may be joined in the same indictment if those charges are founded on the same facts, or form or are part of a series of offences of the same or a similar character. Where the court considers that a defendant may be prejudiced or embarrassed in their defence by reason of being charged with more than one offence in the same indictment, or that for any other reason it is desirable to direct that the defendant should be tried separately for any one or more offences charged in an indictment, it may order a separate trial of any count or counts. Where all the parties want a joint trial, the court should agree to a joint trial. Where both Prosecution and Defence do not want a joint trial, the court should agree to the defendants being tried separately unless it considers that there are good reasons for a joint trial.

Continuity of exhibits

When defending look out for the continuity of the Crown's exhibits. For example, in a drugs case, it is up to the Prosecution to prove that the defendant possessed the controlled drug. This will usually involve sending the drugs to an analyst. The drugs may be seized from the defendant by officer A. Officer A will pass the drugs to officer B for storage. Another officer will take the drugs from storage and send them to the labs. The labs will need to identify which drugs have been analysed. If the passage of the drugs is not absolutely clear and documented you have a cast-iron argument that the chain that shows that the drugs on the defendant are the same drugs that were tested by the labs has been broken.

Similarly, with stolen items, it is often necessary for the original owner to view property taken from the defendant to try to prove that the item found in the defendant's possession was theirs. When an officer takes an item from store to show to a member of the public, the officer must be very careful to demonstrate that what has been taken from police storage is indeed the same object that was taken from the defendant.

Applying for an adjournment

Many cases seem to need a number of adjournments before everything and everyone is ready. The courts are obviously keen to see cases proceed quickly and applications to adjourn generally need to be justified. This is especially true when dealing with District Judges who may force your hand (or attempt to do so) and press on with a case regardless of whether one side says that it is not ready. What follows is a checklist of factors that will influence the likelihood of the court granting an adjournment:

- Whether there have been any previous adjournments, and if so, for what reason.

- Whether there has been any delay in the progress of the case and, if so, whose fault it was.

- The reasons why you are applying for an adjournment. If the point that you are raising could not have been anticipated any earlier and the point is clearly important and relevant then the application should succeed.

You should only apply for an adjournment if it is really necessary or on clear instructions. There is no point in applying for an adjournment to enable an absent witness to attend if it is clear that the witness is probably not going to turn up next time either. Also, if you have a large number of witnesses and one is absent, it may be better to proceed rather than to run the risk of others not turning up in the future.

Take the defendant's instructions on whether they are happy for the case to proceed. You should make clear to the defendant the consequences of adjourning, eg, a delayed trial and an increase in costs. If the defendant is still happy for the case to proceed, you may want to ask them to endorse your brief accordingly to avoid possible misunderstandings over the instructions given.

You should inform the other side that you will be applying for an adjournment as soon as possible and find out whether your application will be opposed. The court is not obliged to grant an adjournment just because the other side does not oppose the application, but obviously it will help if your application is unopposed. If the application is unopposed, it would be a good idea to say so at the outset, by saying, for example:

> Sir, this is an application to adjourn. Might I make it clear at the outset that the Crown supports/does not intend to object to this application.

Before making the application to adjourn you should also consider whether you need to make any other applications, eg, for bail.

Making the application to adjourn

When applying for an adjournment set out your reasons, eg, witness is unable to attend, public funding has only just been granted and/or you have only recently been instructed. Draw the court's attention to the fact that there have been no previous adjournments (if that is the case) or explain why any previous adjournments were granted, emphasising that you did not apply for them or that the reason for applying in the past is not the same as the reason for applying now. Tell the court how long an adjournment is required and have ready a list of dates to avoid.

If the application is opposed, the other party will then address the court. If you are opposing an application, draw to the court's attention any previous applications by the other party to adjourn, the delay caused by such applications and by this application (after all, justice delayed is justice denied), any prejudice or inconvenience you will suffer as a result of an adjournment and the length of time since the offence was committed. If you are defending, stress that the defendant is prejudiced by having a charge hanging over them, eg, when applying for jobs, that they should not be deprived any longer of the chance to prove their innocence and that the charges are stale. If the defendant is in custody, emphasise that they are being denied their liberty and/or livelihood.

Pre-trial review hearing

Most cases set down for trial will go through a pre-trial review hearing unless the case is very straightforward. This is a short administrative hearing that can be conducted by the clerk of the court/legal adviser. There is a form that the court uses to check readiness for trial. Many of the questions are aimed at the same issues as those dealt with in this chapter. The questions that the court will ask in a pre-trial review are:

General
- Has the defendant been advised that credit is offered for pleading guilty?
- Has the Prosecution served advanced disclosure, schedule of unused material and any additional s 9 statements?
- Has the Defence served a defence statement? Will it do so?
- Have alternative disposals been considered (eg, plea bargain)?
- What is the 'bottom line' for the Prosecution in terms of what it would accept by way of pleas to any offence?
- What (if anything) has been offered in terms of plea that has been rejected?

Any special requirements
For example:
- Do audiotapes need to be played?
- Is the master tape required (or will a copy do?)
- Is there any video evidence? If so, what format is it in? Does it need to be played? Is it material and evidential?
- Will the court need to go on a 'site visit'? If so, how long will it take?

Evidence

- Is this a trial of fact only?
- What are the issues in the case?
- What points of law are likely to arise in the trial?
- Are any relevant authorities going to be cited?
- What facts can be reduced into writing using a s 10 of the Criminal Justice Act (CJA) 1967 admission?
- Can any of the prosecution witnesses be agreed by a s 9 of the CJA 1967 statement?
- What are the names of the known witnesses?
- Is any witness summons required?

Witness care

- Do any of the witnesses suffer from a disability requiring any special facilities?
- Do any of the witnesses require an interpreter?
- Are any of the witnesses under 18 years of age?
- Is any witness likely to be intimidated and need:
  - victim support?
  - a pre-trial familiarisation visit?
  - to give evidence from behind a screen?
  - to give evidence from a live TV link?
  - any other provisions?

If there are any outstanding issues (eg, some evidence has not been disclosed) then the court is likely to ask what *directions* might usefully be made by the court to have the outstanding matters sorted out in time for the trial. Plainly, if you are defending, you would want the directions to give the Prosecution as little time as possible to comply with it. This will keep the case moving on, and put pressure on the Prosecution. Should the Prosecution fail to comply with a direction, this could later support any application for an abuse of process.

The final matter is to give the case a listing (ie, a date for the trial). Some courts list more cases in one day than they could possibly hear. This is because a percentage of cases become 'not effective' (for example, because a witness fails to attend or a defendant decides to plead guilty at the last moment) and it would be better to have other work to take. The other side of the coin is that if all the cases in the list are effective, then some cases may have to be adjourned for lack of court time. If there is any reason why the case you are listing for trial should take precedent, and should not be double listed with other cases, then you should make representations at the pre-trial review.

In listing the case for trial the court will seek, from both sides, an idea of how long the case is likely to take. Giving accurate time estimations improves with experience. In practice, the very simple cases (simple road traffic, shoplifting, etc) where there is only really one witness for the Prosecution and the defendant to give evidence, the trial might take an hour or two. Otherwise, consider asking for half a day, or a day according to the number of factual issues and the complexity of the case. Few cases are listed for over a day and the ones that are tend to be the cases where there are multiple defendants.

If the defendant is particularly keen to be represented by a particular person then you may wish to have the availability of that person to hand. It is unlikely that the court would fit a date around a particular person's availability, but it is often the case that the court will moot a couple of dates before deciding upon the best time, and to some extent you can try to influence the court into choosing a date when the preferred advocate is available.

13   Reviewing disclosure

The experience of most advocates is that getting all the necessary information from the prosecuting authority (usually the Crown Prosecution Service) is not an absolutely straightforward matter. The first thing is to understand the duties that are involved.

Duties upon the Prosecution to disclose evidence

The Prosecution has a duty to *serve* the evidence that it will rely upon in trial in any indictable case (any case that could be heard in the Crown Court). The prosecutor has a duty to continue to *review* a case and to serve any information that might undermine the prosecution case (s 3 of the Criminal Procedure and Investigation Act (CPIA) 1996). This is called the duty of 'primary disclosure'.

What might undermine the prosecution case will often depend upon the nature of the defence. If the Prosecution has evidence that would only undermine its case if the defence were put in a certain way, the Prosecution is unlikely to disclose this as primary disclosure.

It is then for the Defence to indicate to the Prosecution what the nature of the defence is. In the Crown Court it is mandatory to reveal something of the defence in a 'defence case statement'. This statement alerts the Prosecution to the nature of the defence, and the Prosecution must review again whether all proper disclosure has been made in light of the stated defence in the case. In the magistrates' court it is not compulsory to file a defence case statement, but if one is *not* served then the Prosecution does *not* need to perform another specific review. This review of disclosure consequent to the defence case statement is called 'secondary disclosure' under s 7 of the CPIA 1996.

An example of the operation of secondary disclosure might be if the defendant says 'it was not me, it was X'. Having named another person as the actual offender, the

Defence would be entitled to any information that might help establish that X was indeed the offender in the case. This information would not be disclosed unless or until the Defence indicated that the defence in the case was going to be blaming X.

There is a further and continuing duty on any prosecutor to review the progress of a case, and to disclose any information that would undermine its case or support the defence case. This is under s 9 of the CPIA 1996.

In summary, the Prosecution's duty is a threefold one:

- Primary disclosure. The Prosecution must serve the evidence on which it will rely and any evidence that undermines its case.

- Secondary disclosure. This is the disclosure of any other evidence that was not thought to be relevant until the Defence stated the nature of the defence to the case.

- Continuing duty to disclose matters that might undermine the prosecution case and strengthen the defence case.

What sort of evidence might the Prosecution have that has not been disclosed?

It is hard to appreciate what it is that you have not been given, but there are certain types of documents that are often not disclosed in primary disclosure but may very well be worth seeing. Here is a list of documents that you might ask the Prosecution to allow you to see:

- The custody record. A custody record is the record of what happened whilst the defendant was in custody having just been arrested. The police have to make decisions about when to conduct an interview and how long to detain a defendant and the decisions taken should be recorded in the custody record. If, for example, the defendant gave an unfavourable interview but says that they were too ill or drunk to answer questions properly, then you will certainly want to review the custody record for evidence of the defendant indeed being ill or drunk.

The custody record will also note the personal possessions of the defendant when booked into custody. Knowing the personal effects of the defendant at the time of arrest can be important in a trial. It may be that it is significant that a defendant was armed or unarmed. It may be relevant to know whether the defendant had any money. The custody record will record these details.

The record will note if any injury was witnessed on the defendant and it will detail whether a police doctor was called to examine them. In assault cases where the defence is one of self-defence, the custody record can be crucial in recording injuries upon the defendant.

The custody record will record the time of interview and state of the defendant between arrest and interview. It will usually give clear indication of whether the defendant was drunk or not. This may also be a relevant issue in a trial.

The custody record will also record whether legal advice was offered and what response the defendant made to the offer of having a solicitor in attendance.

- CRIS (Crime Report Information System) report. This document is a computer printout that logs all activities conducted by police officers in relation to their investigation of the alleged offence. The officers' statements often omit significant parts of the investigation that may prove useful to the defence.

The CRIS report will note when calls are received (and from whom). The transcript for 999 calls is dealt with separately below. You should also find details of the original allegation made and this quite frequently differs from the statements given subsequently by the alleged victim. There will be details of the contact that the officers have had with the witnesses and it will be shown if there has been any reluctance to provide a statement or continue with a complaint (which can be very useful in cross-examination).

- A CAD (Computer Aided Dispatch) report. Whenever a police car calls into the police station a record of the conversation is taken. An example of the value of doing this is when a police car is chasing a suspect vehicle. The officer will give a live radio commentary of what is happening. This helps when the driving is then charged as being careless or dangerous, or where there is an issue as to the identity of the driver.

- Video and CCTV. CCTV has certainly changed the course of crime in public places and has assisted the police to 'clean up' many trouble spots. It has also led to some significant problems with regard to disclosure. The problem stems from the fact that the videotapes which are used to record what the CCTV cameras see are not kept for very long. The tapes are reused often within a matter of days and the evidence is lost.

  In cases involving CCTV video evidence there are regularly arguments at court over whose fault it was that the evidence was lost. I discuss the blame for failure to disclose below.

- 999 call transcripts. All 999 calls made to the police are recorded and can be transcribed. It is often helpful to hear the original in terms of tone of voice, etc, and the words used when first reporting an incident can be useful to know.

- Previous convictions of prosecution witnesses. Do not expect the Prosecution to disclose the previous convictions of its witnesses unless you specifically ask. If the defendant too has previous convictions you may feel that it is most unwise to bring up the issue of character in a case. You may wish to see the list of previous convictions before you make your mind up. In any case of violence where the defence is self-defence, a defence advocate would want to see whether the prosecution witnesses have histories of violence. In any case where the defence may involve accusations that the prosecution witnesses are liars then it would be helpful to know whether they have been convicted for matters of dishonesty.

Failing to disclose – who is to blame?

Many cases become delayed because the trial is listed before all the disclosure is made. Benches understandably get very annoyed when a trial has to be put back because the Prosecution and Defence are still arguing about disclosure.

There are duties upon both Prosecution and Defence in relation to disclosure. The Prosecution has the higher duty to review the case and disclose any material that may assist the defence case, but the Defence has the opportunity to make it clear what it wants. The Prosecution will be fast to blame the Defence if the first request for information of a particular kind comes on the day of trial!

Best practice is for the Defence to review its case early and thoroughly and write to the Prosecution with a 'shopping list' of any information that it wants. This can go along with a defence case statement or simply a letter.

If the case has not been reviewed well, and the proceedings have advanced some way before the disclosure issue becomes apparent, then you need to be prepared to argue who is to blame.

The way to approach this issue is to consider how obvious it is that the item should be disclosed according to the prosecutor's duty of primary disclosure, or the duty to review generally. The primary duty is to disclose anything that might undermine the prosecution case (or assist the Defence). There is, of course, the issue of whether the defence case has been expressed in a defence case statement, but this is *not* the *only* determinative feature. The defendant may have expressed what the nature of their defence was on arrest and/or in interview.

In some cases defendants even specify in interview the precise document or evidence that would be relevant to the case. For example a defendant could say, 'I was not alone, you will see from the CCTV that I was with my girlfriend!' It would be open to argue that the defendant has expressed the nature of his defence and has put the Prosecution on notice of what evidence should be collected and served by the Prosecution. Each case will depend upon its own facts, but look for evidence of the police/Prosecution being on notice of the nature of the defence and of the documents that would therefore form part of the Prosecution's duty to disclose.

Asking for disclosure – keep a record

If you are defending and, at any point in proceedings, you ask for an adjournment for the Prosecution to serve evidence upon the Defence – make a very clear record of what was requested. It is common to find that requests are not acted upon in time or at all, and it is always useful for those appearing in later hearings to know in detail what was said about disclosure earlier on in proceedings.

It is important to note if the prosecutor accepted the relevance of the document and offered to disclose it. Once one prosecutor has accepted the burden upon the Prosecution to disclose some particular evidence, it is much harder for a subsequent prosecutor to deny the relevance of the evidence and deny that the Prosecution has a duty to disclose the evidence at all.

The remedy for failing to disclose

The Defence will always argue that no trial of a case can start until disclosure has been made. Otherwise, the defendant suffers a procedural unfairness, and the trial would be an abuse of process. It is therefore beholden upon both parties to attempt to ensure that disclosure issues are dealt with before the trial is listed to commence. If the trial is listed and disclosure remains outstanding then one party or other is potentially facing trouble.

If the Defence holds up the trial by raising a disclosure issue on the day of trial, then the court may either refuse an adjournment for the disclosure to be made, or allow the adjournment but penalise the Defence in costs for the wasted time.

If the Defence notified the Prosecution in good time of the disclosure issue and the Prosecution has failed to act in time for the trial, then the court may either adjourn (with or without ordering wasted costs) or refuse to adjourn. If the court refuses to adjourn, the issue arises of whether the trial would be fair or not. If the disclosure was properly sought and is genuinely relevant, then it would not be hard to argue that the trial cannot proceed without it, and to do so would be an abuse of process. If this argument is accepted, then the Prosecution has no option but to offer no evidence at trial (in which event the case is dismissed). The alternative is that the Defence makes an application that there has been an abuse of process (in which event the case could be dismissed).

An example of failure to disclose

Imagine a case where an officer makes a statement accusing the defendant of being very drunk and this is relevant to the charge and to the trial. The defendant was interviewed quite soon after arrest and the Defence suspects that the officer is exaggerating the drunken state of the defendant. To that end, on the first hearing of the case the Defence requests sight of the custody record to glean any information about the defendant's state whilst in custody. The prosecutor on the first occasion does not oppose serving the custody record of the defendant. The case is adjourned for two weeks.

When the case returns to court, the custody record has not yet been served. The Defence can quote that the issue was properly raised on the first occasion and so the court criticises the Prosecution and orders disclosure within seven days. The trial is listed in 21 days. In seven days the Defence has still not seen the custody record. Indeed the day of trial comes, and there is no custody record.

The Prosecution asks to adjourn the trial in order to discover what has happened to the custody record and to serve a copy on the Defence. The Defence opposes the application, and says that the Prosecution has been given ample time to disclose the custody record. The court agrees with the Defence and no adjournment is granted.

If the Prosecution concedes that no fair trial can take place because the Defence has not seen the custody record, it cannot commence a trial and it is forced to offer no evidence. If the Prosecution attempts to proceed to trial without the custody record, the Defence should then submit that to do so would constitute an abuse of process. The application would be bound to succeed unless the Prosecution can argue that the custody record really could not be relevant for the defence advocate to see regardless of what it said. It would be hard for the Prosecution to take this line since it offered to disclose the evidence at the first hearing.

14 Summary trial

This chapter reviews the procedure at trial and gives some ideas for the techniques that an advocate might use in their advocacy.

Pre-trial conference with the defendant

If you are defending and you have not met the defendant before, you should be mindful that the defendant might not be expecting a new representative at trial. The defendant may be quite nervous and you need to settle any anxieties that they may have. Seeing another lawyer for the first time on the day of trial can be quite unnerving for a defendant.

It would probably be a good idea to tackle this upfront. If you are counsel, you can say in your introduction that you are a barrister and that the solicitors have hired you for the case as a specialist advocate. This should sound positive. If you are a solicitor you will probably know the solicitor whose case it is and you can tell the client that X has briefed you very well.

If your instructions are not complete, it is best not to tell this to the defendant. Rather than simply asking for information (which makes you look unprepared) say to the defendant that you want to hear them explain something 'in their own words'.

Think carefully whether a sketch plan or diagram would help you understand the case better.

You may want to clarify whether the defendant still wishes to contest the charges. It may be that the reality of getting to trial makes the defendant review their position. If you are going to advise that the case against the defendant is strong, be careful not to give the impression that you are reluctant to do the trial. Ideally the defendant should believe that you are very keen to fight on their behalf.

Most defendants appreciate being told how the trial will proceed. If the defendant has previous convictions, they may be familiar with the trial process, but it would almost always be a good idea either to talk the defendant through the procedure or at least offer to do so. If the defendant is going to give evidence (or is likely to) tell them to speak slowly and clearly and to keep any answers short and to the point. If the defendant does not know the answer to any question, tell them to say so and not make one up. On the other hand, the defendant should not be evasive. Tell the defendant to keep calm and not to get angry when being cross-examined.

You are not permitted to coach the defendant, or indeed any witness. Coaching is suggesting to the witness or telling the witness what it is that they might say to any answer. Telling the witness that they are going to be asked about an issue X is fine. Telling them what they ought to say about issue X is not.

Talking to the prosecutor before trial

You may have been instructed to offer a part plea or a plea on a basis (see Chapter 10) and you will need to discuss this with the prosecutor. It may be better strategy to find out if the Crown Prosecution Service (CPS) is ready to start the trial before you make any offers at all. It may be that the witnesses have not arrived. It may be that there has been an error in warning witnesses to attend, or that there is some other reason why the prosecutor cannot proceed (see 'Applying for an adjournment if the trial is not ready', p 140).

If the Defence wants to dispute the admissibility of any evidence the prosecutor should be notified as soon as possible. The Defence should also give the prosecutor a copy of any authorities on which it seeks to rely. Copies should also be made for the clerk/legal adviser and the magistrates.

Introductions

At the beginning of a trial the defendant will enter the dock and will be asked by the clerk/legal adviser to confirm their name and address. The clerk/legal adviser will usually introduce the parties or may simply say, 'The defendant is represented by Miss Green'. At this stage, the defence advocate may wish to acknowledge the magistrates, for example by nodding in their direction or by saying, 'Good morning, Sir/Madam'. If the defendant has pleaded not guilty, the clerk/legal adviser will inform the court and the prosecutor will open the case (see below). If the defendant has not already formally entered a not guilty plea, the charge will be put to them so that a not guilty plea can be entered.

If the defendant requires an interpreter, the interpreter will stand next to the defendant in the dock and will take the interpreter's oath before the start of the trial.

Overview of a summary trial

The Prosecution is entitled to make an opening speech before calling its evidence. If there is more than one defendant, the first defendant's advocate will cross-examine the prosecution witnesses before the second defendant's advocate. When the Prosecution has called all its evidence, the Defence can make a submission of no case to answer (see 'Submission of no case to answer', p 136). If no submission is made or if the submission fails, the Defence will then call its evidence. If there is more than one defendant, the second defendant's advocate will cross-examine before the Prosecution.

At the close of the defendant's case the defence advocate will make a closing speech. If there is more than one defendant, the first defendant's advocate will make a closing speech first, after all the evidence has been heard. The Prosecution does not make a closing speech but is entitled to address the court on any questions of law.

Preliminary issues or a *voir dire*

If there is evidence that the Defence thinks is inadmissible, the first thing to do is to check with the prosecutor to see whether they agree. If there is agreement then the prosecutor must remove the evidence and take reasonable steps to ensure that the evidence is not admitted in trial.

If there is no consensus between the two advocates, the next decision is when you should raise the matter with the court. There are two views about the best time to raise a point. Say, for example, that there is an interview which is disputed by the defence advocate on the basis that it should be ruled inadmissible for breach of the Police and Criminal Evidence Act 1984 (PACE). It may be that the prosecutor is intending to make reference to the disputed evidence in their opening speech, and therefore there is some logic in hearing the dispute on admissibility first so that there is a ruling on admissibility before the case begins in earnest and before the prosecutor alludes to evidence in opening.

The counter view is that since the magistrates hear the evidence before they rule it as being admissible or inadmissible, then there is no detriment in the Prosecution opening the case with evidence that may later be ruled as inadmissible. It is one of the weaknesses of the system that benches hear all the evidence, even that evidence which they may go on to rule to be inadmissible. The magistrates are bound to be affected by hearing the evidence, no matter how much they try to put any evidence that they have ruled as inadmissible from their minds.

The only sure guidance about when to take a point on admissibility is to suggest that if the disputed evidence is so fundamental to the prosecution case that the Prosecution would collapse if the evidence was ruled out, it would seem preferable to tackle the issue at the outset of the trial.

Prosecution opening speech

The prosecution opening speech is usually short; sometimes, if the case is very straightforward, the prosecutor will not make an opening speech at all. It should set out a summary of the facts and of any relevant law if necessary. It is worth taking a note of the opening speech. Sometimes the prosecutor will tell the court about evidence which never actually emerges in the trial. A good trial advocate will make a note of any inconsistencies between the case that the prosecutor promised they could present and what was actually presented. The inconsistencies can be used in the Defence closing speech. For example:

> You may recall that this case was opened on the basis that there was evidence of punches and kicking. In fact, you heard no evidence at all of any kicks in this case. This is typical of the uncertainty of the Crown's own case ...

Examination-in-chief

The aim of examination-in-chief is to elicit from your witness evidence establishing and supporting your case. Whereas in cross-examination the advocate will want to control the witness, in examination-in-chief the witness should be allowed to give their version of events freely and with no unnecessary interruptions. However, the advocate should always retain some control, eg, over witnesses straying from the point. What follows are some techniques and tools that you might find useful when approaching examination-in-chief:

- *Leading*

  The general rule is that there should be no leading questions in examination-in-chief. Like all the best rules, there are exceptions. It is generally good practice to lead on the basic uncontroversial facts. If all the prosecution witnesses have said that the event took place on 5 November and the defendant agrees that the event took place on 5 November there is no need at all to avoid leading on the date.

  By the end of the prosecution case it should be very plain which facts are agreed and which are in dispute. Indeed it is often the case that a trial begins to accelerate as the essence of the factual dispute becomes clear and all parties become increasingly confident in leading on the issues that are not controversial.

- *Not leading*

  The great bulk of examination-in-chief should be made up of questions that do not suggest the answer in the question. The general way to accomplish this is to ask questions that start with the words, 'How' 'What' 'Why' 'Where' 'Who' 'When'. This formulation tends to let the witness supply the answer.

  Questions that start 'Did' are more dangerous, since what will normally follow the word 'Did' is a statement that the witness is asked to comment upon. For example, 'Did the man then hit you?' This is a proposition, and the advocate, not the witness, has raised the idea that someone hit someone. Let the witness give the information by asking a question such as 'What did the man do?' Questions that start with 'Did' can be essential, usually not to establish a fact in the case, but to clarify whether the witness can take the evidence any further, eg:

  > Q: What was happening outside?
  >
  > A: There were two men shouting.
  >
  > Q: Do you recall what they were shouting about?

  The last of those questions is not suggesting the answer but just checking whether there is any more evidence to explore.

  Simple questions are almost always best. When used at the right time with the right emphasis, one of the most devastatingly effective questions in examination-in-chief is simply 'Why?'

- *Separate the issues from the chronology*

  The easiest way for any tribunal to take in an account of an incident is if the incident is related chronologically. You should be quite strong in telling the witness how you would like the evidence. For example:

  > Could I ask you to explain step by step what you recall of what you saw take place between Smith and Jones.

By asking for the account 'step by step' or 'stage by stage' you are asking for a chronology. You can maintain this with questions such as:

> At what stage did that happen?
>
> How long did that take place for?

Hopefully you will only need to ask a few questions in this way before the witness understands from you that the account should be very carefully ordered and chronological.

Given that you are looking to establish a clear order of events, it is best if you do not interrupt the chronological flow with other evidence. For example, it may be important to know about lighting conditions in an identification case. It is much better to establish the lighting conditions, etc, before you get the witness to deal with the sequence of events. This is really just setting the scene ahead of the action. You should do this clearly, eg:

> Before I ask you about 5 November itself, could I ask you to describe the Faint Rat public house?

There may be several items of scene setting that would be necessary to make the subsequent chronology run more smoothly.

- *Insulating a witness*

The advocate should also 'insulate' the witness from cross-examination. Many junior practitioners think that if there is a weakness in a case it is best left alone. This is rarely a good idea since your opponent will not leave the weakness alone, and if you leave it alone then you are effectively leaving an open door for your opponent.

There are basically three situations to consider. The first is where there is an evident weakness in your case. The witness has an explanation, but it is not a very good one. In this situation it would be best to allow the witness to explain themselves in examination-in-chief. It is by far the best opportunity to allow the witness to tackle the weak area of the account and to do their very best to lessen the impact of the cross-examination by dealing with the problem upfront.

The second situation is where the weakness is subtler and you are not sure that the other side will notice it. In these circumstances you will have to look at the odds. If the point is seen and taken then you may be in a worse position for not having allowed the witness to deal with it in the relative comfort of examination-in-chief. If the point is not spotted then you will do well not to raise the point of your own volition.

The third situation is where there is a weakness and the witness is absolutely dreadful and incomprehensible when trying to explain their behaviour in regard to this point. You may take the view that you will not be able to get any sense out of the defendant and you are just going to leave the point for your opponent to struggle with.

- *Don't comment*

  You may not mean to pass any comment, but an incidental remark such as 'thank you', 'I see', 'right', 'good', or 'OK' can be construed as comment. Even if the remark is incidental it is likely to irritate the court. Therefore, saying 'OK', etc, is irritating at best and professionally objectionable as comment at worst.

- *Let the defendant comment on the prosecution case*

  The defendant has heard the whole case. It is generally wrong to ask witnesses to comment upon each other, but in the case of the defendant this can be necessary for the sake of clarity. The court needs to know exactly what the defendant's response is to the allegations.

  Let the defendant give their account *without* reference to the prosecution case first and *at the end* put the actual allegations clearly and directly. For example:

You have heard that the Crown alleges that you threw the first punch. What do you say about that?

This is not a leading question. The question is 'What do you say about that?' which does not suggest the answer.

Introducing exhibits

Exhibits are real evidence, ie objects produced for inspection in order that the court may draw inferences from its examination of them. Exhibits must be produced and identified by the relevant witnesses.

When you reach the point in the evidence where it is necessary and helpful to see the exhibit, pass the exhibit up to the witness. Ask the witness what the object is. Having identified the object you may ask the bench to receive the object as an exhibit in the case. It is normally correct and courteous for the Defence to let the Prosecution know if it intends to produce any exhibits. If the prosecutor is caught unaware that the Defence has an exhibit, it is conceivable that all the prosecution witnesses will need to be recalled to comment upon this evidence and this would have costs implications.

Dealing with interviews

In court the prosecutor will read out the agreed transcript of interview or play the tape-recording if the summary is inaccurate or there is some other reason why it would be better to listen to the original recording. If a police officer is giving evidence, it is common practice for the officer to read out the questions and for the prosecutor to read out the defendant's answers. This is to help the court follow the interview more easily.

Under s 34 of the Criminal Justice and Public Order Act 1994 the court can draw adverse inferences from the fact that the defendant did not answer questions at interview. If you are defending and the defendant has given a 'no comment' interview, ask the defendant beforehand why they did so and deal with it when examining-in-chief. If they have a good reason, eg, a solicitor advised the defendant to do so, you may on rare occasions need to call the solicitor who advised the defendant to explain why that advice was given. Remember to address the court on whether adverse inferences should be drawn from the defendant's silence in the closing speech.

Before any inference can be drawn from failing to answer questions in interview, the police need to explain the caution fully. Ideally the police officer would say something along the following lines:

> You are currently declining to answer questions. I should remind you that this could prove important in any later trial. If you are asked the same question at trial that I am asking you now and you give an answer, the court is bound to wonder why you didn't answer the question now. Do you want to reconsider whether you wish to answer the question why you had the knife with you?

Some officers are not so fulsome in explaining the consequences of not answering questions in interview, and if the defendant gives a 'no comment' interview the Defence should always listen to the tape to hear how the officer actually warned the defendant about maintaining silence. If the explanation is short and inadequate the Defence can properly cross-examine the officer about the quality of the warning and then submit in the closing speech that an adverse inference is not proper.

Police referring to notebooks or statements

Police officers are not expected to recall all the incidents that they attend, and the general rule is that they are allowed to have their notes before them to refresh their memory.

If the note was made at the time, or very close to the time of the incident, the rule is that this is better evidence than if it were made a day or so later. The better the quality of the note, the more likely it is that the court will allow the officer to refer to it.

It is very rare for the Defence to challenge an application for an officer to refer to notes. What is more likely to be problematic is when the officer just starts reading those notes out. The purpose of the note is to help memory and recall, *not to replace it*. If the officer simply starts reading out, the Defence should object. This might go as follows:

> Sir, I hesitate to interrupt but it seems that the officer is intending simply to read out his/her notes. Might he/she be reminded that evidence should come from his/her memory wherever possible?

Hostile witnesses

A hostile witness is one who appears to be deliberately not co-operating with the party who has called them, eg, by refusing to answer questions or giving evidence inconsistent with an earlier statement.

If a prosecution witness turns hostile and refuses to answer questions as expected, the prosecutor may make an application to in effect cross-examine their own witness and to encourage the witness to accept the contents of their earlier witness statement.

The Defence can object to such an application. If the witness gives some answers that are helpful to the Prosecution, the Defence can argue that the witness is not truly hostile. It is just bad luck for the prosecutor that the witness is not saying everything that the prosecutor had hoped. However, if there are no helpful answers at all, the bench is likely to allow the prosecutor to treat the witness as hostile. The Defence may seek to argue that the witness has just thought better of all the lies they told in their statement but be careful one of the main reasons that a prosecution witness turns 'hostile' to the prosecution is that the defendant has threatened them!

Summary for examination-in-chief

When examining-in-chief:

- Start by asking the witness to give their name, occupation, professional address, etc.

- You may want to set the scene by asking the witness to describe the layout of the room, street, etc, in some detail. If appropriate, ask the witness to estimate distances by reference to the size of the courtroom.

- Except where the subject matter is not in dispute, do not ask leading questions, eg, 'Were the trainers a size nine?' but ask instead, 'What size were the trainers?'

- Use phrases such as 'Describe ...', 'What happened on ...?' to start and continue the story-telling, and then try to keep the witness chronological where possible.

- Keep questions short and simple and use plain English.

- Use changes in pace, eg, pause after a favourable answer to give emphasis.

- If the witness is giving evidence too quickly, tell them to slow down so that the clerk/legal adviser is able to take a note of everything that is said.

- Keep the witness to relevant evidence. Be clear in what you are asking for.

- You need to check that the relevant detail has been given. If the witness misses the detail, ask for it (without leading). For example 'Can you describe what you mean by that?' or 'What words did he actually use?' or 'How tall?'.

- Ask about matters which you know weaken your case rather than waiting for them to be brought up in cross-examination, when the impact will be greater.

- Try not to ask questions to which you do not know the answer. The answer may be unfavourable to your case and cause irreparable damage.

- Ask an expert witness about their qualifications and experience, refer the expert to their report and then ask the expert about the other side's expert's report (if there is one).

- Take a note of as much of the witness's evidence as possible, as you may wish to refer to what they said later in the trial, eg, in your final speech.

- Do not comment on or repeat a witness's answers.

Cross-examination

Cross-examination is the process of examining your opponent's witnesses. The aim of cross-examination is first, to 'put your case' to the witness and secondly, to undermine your opponent's case. Cases can be won on a skilful cross-examination, but if you ask the wrong questions or one question too many the results can be disastrous.

You are *not* looking to hear much more evidence from the witness. The focus should now be on you, as *you* communicate your case to the witness and the court. If you are defending, you need to make the defendant's position plain and so you want the witness to say as little as possible. To that end, you want to ask leading questions which require nothing more than a 'yes' or 'no' answer.

The general technique is that you should use facts to build your conclusions. Pick the facts in the case that tend to support the conclusion that you want to make. You must give yourself the best chance of establishing the conclusion in your favour by building to the conclusion with the facts. It is much less effective to start with the conclusion and then try to justify it later.

For example, imagine the prosecution witness has seen the defendant 'eyeing up' a girl in a nightclub. Your conclusion is that it was very hard to make a accurate observation of what the defendant was doing. The technique is to ask leading questions to keep the witness's answers short and to use the facts to build to a conclusion. For example, you could say:

Q:	You had been in the club for four hours already that night, hadn't you?
A:	Yes.
Q:	And you had been drinking beer.
A:	That's right.
Q:	You must have been tired as you were at work all day beforehand.
A:	I was a bit tired but not too bad.
Q:	The club was busy that night.
A:	Yes.
Q:	And there was strobe lighting.
A:	Yes, some of the time.
Q:	You were with friends of your own whom you were talking to.
A:	Yes.
Q:	And you were not watching the defendant all the time.
A:	No.
Q:	You got the impression that the defendant was 'eyeing up' your girlfriend as you described.
A:	I certainly did.
Q:	But it was very difficult in those circumstances to be sure what it was that the defendant was doing.
A:	I thought that he was looking at my girlfriend.

In the example above, the advocate has really just made a series of statements. These statements make up the defence case, and so you can see that cross-examination is a combination of asking questions and putting one's case. It is generally better to ask very little and concentrate on the case that you must put on the basis of facts that you know. Your primary focus is generally not to let the witness give more evidence, but for you to communicate your case to the court by the case that you put to the witness.

In the example, the conclusion is that the circumstances made it hard to be sure about what was seen. It is important to be realistic and not to expect a witness to agree with you. The objective is to make that conclusion appear as plausible as possible *to the court*. The best method for this is to accumulate all the facts that tend to support that conclusion, and put them in turn to lead the witness and the court towards the conclusion. The witness may then feel compelled to agree with the conclusion in part and this is likely to be as good as you are going to get.

Once you have made the point, it is rarely a good idea to pursue it. As a general rule, witnesses improve the quality of their replies the more you press. Take the example above. The witness has not denied that it would be hard to see properly. He has reasserted his opinion, but that opinion has probably been undermined a little by virtue of the questions that lead up to the conclusion. If the advocate pushed the matter further, there could be a catastrophe! For example (starting with the last question and answer):

Q: But it was very difficult in those circumstances to be sure what it was that the defendant was doing.

A: I thought that he was looking at my girlfriend.

Q: But you can't be sure, can you?

A: I certainly felt sure.

Q: But you may have been wrong given the lighting and so forth.

A: I am not wrong.

Q: But you can't be 100% sure.

A: I am 100% sure.

The additional questions have basically erased the doubts that the witness might have had after the factual build up. It is right that the witness *might* have agreed and said that he was not sure, and that would have been good for the defence. If you have a really strong point *and* a reasonable witness, then you *might* risk the 'but you can't be sure' question. If you are in any doubt, *do not risk repeating the question*. Strike once and then leave the point alone. Pressing the point will often only destroy it. You will have an opportunity to have the last word in your speech. Press the point home then.

When cross-examining:

- Use leading questions and think of ways of causing the most impact. Plan your cross-examination as much as possible in advance, and in particular, have ready your first and last questions.

- Make sure you are clear as to exactly what your case is. Have a strong mental picture of the events as described by your witnesses and communicate the case to the court via the witness. Although you can say, 'I put it to you that ...', your questions will have greater impact if you simply state your point in the form of a question, eg, 'You couldn't see what really happened, could you?' You should put to a witness any part of your case that is in dispute and on which the witness can comment.

- There may be points in the witness's evidence which concur with your version of events and which will support your case. Encourage agreement where possible. For example, a witness may agree that a place is crowded or that street lighting is poor. If such points will assist you, then bring them out in cross-examination.

- Decide if a witness can expand on something that may be helpful, but be careful if you do not know what the answer to a question is going to be: an unexpected answer could be extremely damaging.

- Look for gaps in the evidence where the witness is silent about something that they would have mentioned had it been damaging to your case. It may be that the witness has deliberately left it out.

- Highlight any events that the witness failed to see or hear but which you would have expected the witness to see or hear if the whole incident had been witnessed. This is particularly important when you are dealing with evidence that is unfavourable to your case, as it will instil doubt in the minds of the magistrates about evidence that had seemed strong and clear.

- Look out for inconsistencies between witnesses, and, where you have been given a copy of a witness statement, highlight any differences between the statement and the live evidence, in order to discredit the witness.

- If a witness starts crying or becomes emotional, pause to allow the witness to regain their composure before continuing. Do not lose the court's sympathy by being insensitive.

- If you are defending a defendant who is not of 'good character', be careful when cross-examining prosecution witnesses not to involve imputations on the character of the witnesses as the defendant may lose their shield and their character may then be put in evidence.

- Where possible, take a note of the answers that a witness gives as you may wish to refer to them later in the trial, eg, in closing.

- Look for any reason why the witness may be giving evidence for the other party, eg, they are related, best friends, or work colleagues. Draw attention to any potential reasons for bias. This is especially so with alibi witnesses.

Re-examination

The general rule is: don't! However, re-examination may be necessary, eg, to limit any damage done to your case by your witness's answers in cross-examination. This might arise, for example, if the witness when cross-examined has given evidence of only part of a conversation favourable to the cross-examiner's case and the other part of the conversation is favourable to the examiner-in-chief's case. The purpose of re-examination is to clarify and explain answers given in cross-examination. When you re-examine, you are only entitled to ask questions arising from your opponent's cross-examination. You cannot introduce any new matters, so make sure you remember to ask everything you want to in-chief. As with examination-in-chief, do not ask leading questions.

When you have finished re-examining and the magistrates have asked any questions, you should ask for your witness to be released.

Concluding the prosecution case

After dealing with live witnesses, the prosecutor will read through any s 9 statements. These are statements which have been served on the Defence which the Defence has agreed to being read out because the evidence is not in dispute, eg, a loser's statement in a theft case, a doctor's statement in an assault case where the defence is self-defence and a police officer's statement which only confirms their presence during an interview.

When the prosecutor has adduced all the evidence that the prosecutor relies on to prove their case, they will say:

'That concludes the case for the Prosecution' or 'that is the Crown's case'.

The Defence indicates the close of its case in the same way.

Submission of no case to answer

At the close of the prosecution case, the Defence has the opportunity of making a submission of no case to answer. This is often called a 'half-time' submission since it is made after one of the two parties has called its evidence.

The reason for having an opportunity to challenge the case against the defendant is based on a defendant's fundamental rights. The right that the defendant enjoys is that they should not be called to account, nor asked to justify their actions if there is no real basis for an accusation being made in the first place.

Having heard the prosecution case, you have essentially two ways of persuading the court that it should dismiss the case at this stage. These two ways derive from *Practice Direction (Submission of No Case)* [1962] 1 WLR 227.

The first way is to argue that there is *no* evidence of an essential element of the offence. The word 'no' connotes a very high burden upon the Defence if it is to succeed under this head. An example of where an application under this limb of the test might succeed is in a theft case where there is no evidence that the defendant acted dishonestly. Usually when a person complains that an item has been stolen from them, they will add at the end of their statement that nobody had permission to take any item from them. This may seem self-evident, but technically if there is no evidence that an appropriation was not *permitted* by the victim in a case then the Defence may submit that the Prosecution has no evidence of dishonesty and therefore of theft. It is rare to argue that there has been no evidence of an element of an offence.

The second way is more widely drawn. It states that the case should be dismissed if the evidence is so manifestly unreliable or discredited in cross-examination that no reasonable tribunal could convict upon it. The test is not a statutory test and the *Practice Direction* is not the only source of the test. There is the case of *R v Galbraith* [1981] 1 WLR 1039 too which discusses the test for submissions of no case to answer. Since *Galbraith* deals with the position in relation to juries, it is preferred in the Crown Court whilst the *Practice Direction* is preferred in the magistrates' court.

The essence of the second way is simply that where the Prosecution has some evidence, but the quality of that evidence is so poor that it could never amount to evidence on which a tribunal could convict, then the case should not proceed further.

The advantage of making a submission of no case to answer is that it allows for a review to be made of the weaknesses of the prosecution case before the court is aware of any weaknesses that may be shown in due course in the defence case.

Some advocates are wary about making submissions of no case, since the test is quite a difficult one to fulfil. This is in contrast to the closing speech, where the burden is firmly upon the Prosecution. The fear of some advocates is that if the Defence makes its best points and has them refused on a submission of no case, the same points seem less forceful when argued a second time at the conclusion of a trial. It is certainly right that a closing speech will be less forceful if it is a repetition of the submission of no case to answer, but the advocate must weigh up this disadvantage with the chance of having the case dismissed before the potential pitfall of having to call the defendant to give evidence.

The decision to make the application is a matter of judgment.

Defence closing speech

Most magistrates' court trials are not especially long, and there is little need to remind the court of the evidence. It is more useful for the Defence to collect parts of the evidence together in order to comment upon its reliability and strength. Common sense is a strong ally in any closing speech, and it is persuasive and helpful to indicate where evidence in your favour appears to support common sense, and where the prosecution evidence fails to comport with common sense.

It is permissible to comment upon the demeanour of a witness and the manner in which the witness answered questions. It may be that a witness simply did or did not sound as if they were telling the truth. Whilst the advocate is permitted to make observations about the witness this should be undertaken with great care so as not to overstep the mark. Magistrates are not easily persuaded that prosecution witnesses are liars and it may offend the magistrates if a witness is criticised too aggressively by an advocate.

Be careful not to try too hard to prove the defence case in a closing speech. There is *generally* no burden on the Defence to prove its case, and if an advocate attempts to prove too much, they may lose credibility in the court's eyes. Such a loss of credibility can be avoided by simply not trying to prove matters that do not require proof. The only requirement in the great majority of cases is for the Prosecution to prove its case so that the court is sure of the defendant's guilt. The only caveat to this being the rule in all cases is that the law *occasionally* requires the defendant to prove an element of the defence case. This is called a 'reverse burden'. Reverse burden cases are rare. An example would be the requirement on a defendant to prove that they had lawful authority for the possession of a bladed article (s 139 of the Criminal Justice Act 1988).

The defence closing speech should contain:

- A summary of the defence case. Do not be repetitive or tedious, but also be careful not to take too much for granted. There may be members of a lay bench who have had very little experience of court.

- A summary of the weaknesses in the prosecution case.

- Any answers to questions in cross-examination that prosecution witnesses gave which suggest that the defendant is not guilty.

- An explanation of any evidence which damages the defence case, eg, that the prosecution witness is mistaken.

- If addressing a lay bench on the law or a District Judge on an unusual point, an explanation of the applicable law.

- If addressing a lay bench, a short reminder of the burden and standard of proof, eg, that when deciding whether to convict, it is not a question of whether they prefer the prosecution or the defence case but whether they are sure beyond reasonable doubt that the prosecution case is proved.

Applying for an adjournment if the trial is not ready

See 'Applying for an adjournment', p 105.

Prosecutors

Most of what has been discussed is relevant to both parties. Prosecutors have a slightly different set of options on what to do if a witness does not attend. The first thing to do is to speak to the police liaison officer, or better still to one of the officers appearing as a witness if there is such a person at court. The police can often arrange for a police car to be sent to the address of a witness who has not attended and find out why.

Prosecutors should be careful about talking to witnesses before trial. The rules against coaching are strict, and it is safest to do no more than to greet the witnesses, give them copies of their statements to refresh their memory and to tell the witnesses what is happening in terms of procedure. If the witness gives inadmissible evidence in the statement, it is advisable to warn the witness not to repeat this evidence. It is also a good idea to encourage the witnesses to offer eye contact to the magistrates.

What if ...?

- *The magistrates refuse to adjourn a trial when one party is not ready?*

If the application to adjourn was made by the Prosecution and was refused by the court, the prosecutor has to decide whether it is possible and fair to proceed with the trial. Remember that the ethical position is not to attempt to secure a conviction at all costs. If a prosecution witness is not essential to the prosecution, but is essential to the defence, it is not right to proceed with the trial. Contact the CPS representative and ask for permission to 'offer no evidence' because witnesses have failed to attend and the application to adjourn was refused.

If defence witnesses have failed to attend and the bench has refused to grant an adjournment, then proceed with the trial and consider an appeal if the Defence loses the case.

15 Sentencing

What is a pre-sentence report?

At the sentencing stage, the court has the option of calling upon the probation service to write a report about the defendant to assist the court in selecting the suitable sentence.

A pre-sentence report is a report written by the probation service to help the sentencing court with an assessment of the offender. The report is to assist the court with an unbiased and frank appraisal of such things as the following:

- how the offender feels about the offence;
- any remorse that the offender may have shown;
- the likelihood of re-offending;
- the risk posed by the offender to the community;
- the possible benefits of any particular sentence to the behaviour of the offender.

The report will contain a review of the case and the offender's reaction to the offence of which they have been convicted. This could easily be done by the defendant's advocate, but the court will generally prefer to hear from a probation officer since the officer is able to speak freely and is not bound to say what is favourable to the offender.

The report will contain some form of assessment of the offender in terms of the likelihood of re-offending. It is perfectly possible for this assessment to be negative to the offender, and to assess them as high risk. The assessment is a matter of opinion, and the advocate is entitled to challenge it although the probation officer should have some expertise in the matter.

The conclusion of the report will examine the sentences that the probation service could administer and will consider whether, in the view of the probation service, such an option might be effective.

Ready to sentence or adjourn for reports?

Whenever the defendant pleads guilty or is convicted, there is the question of whether to sentence directly, or to ask for the case to be adjourned for the preparation of a pre-sentence report (PSR).

The court will need to consult the probation service before passing any sentence that would be administered by the service. Even if the court decides not to pass a sentence administered by the probation service, the court will usually want the benefit of the report and of the options that it contains before deciding. This is the case in all but the most minor cases. If the case is serious enough for public funding to have been granted, one would normally expect the court to order a report.

How long will it take?

The reports generally take four weeks if the defendant is on bail, and three weeks if in custody. Different probation areas have greater or lesser workloads at any given time, and the probation officer will advise the court on whether the report could be written more swiftly or whether there is a particular backlog and more time than usual would be needed.

What kind of report?

There are several types of reports. The most common is the 'all options' report. This simply means that the court asks the probation service to be aware that the court is also considering custody as a sentencing option. Any 'all options' PSR should contain an assessment of the likely effect of a custodial sentence on the offender.

If the court is satisfied that the case does not warrant a custodial sentence, the court can order a 'community penalty' PSR, which will only detail the suitability of sentences in the community administered by the probation service.

Advocacy in the Magistrates' Court

Specific sentence reports

Sometimes the court has a particular community penalty in mind, but there is no PSR. Rather than adjourning for a PSR, the court can ask the probation officer at court to see the defendant right away and report back to the court. The probation officer is usually asked to consider a single question/issue, eg, 'is the defendant suitable for a community punishment order?' The hope is that the probation officer can see the defendant and report back to the court with an answer as soon as possible, preferably the same day, and that the court may then proceed to sentence without delay.

Asking for a PSR

The court will normally grant an application for a PSR with little hesitation. Make it clear which sort of PSR you are asking for. Only ask for a community penalty PSR if the case is such that custody would not seem to be an appropriate sentence on any reasonable interpretation of the case.

If the court has just heard a guilty plea, the next stage is for the Prosecution to outline the facts of the case. If the case is clearly not a trivial one, some advocates try to avoid the necessity of having the Prosecution give an opening of the facts by indicating straight away that there is an application for a pre-sentence report. The application might be along the following lines:

> Sir, before the Prosecution opens the facts of the case, might I indicate that the Defence would ask the court to consider adjourning the case for a pre-sentence report. This is a case of possession of Class A drugs, and in my submission any sentencing court would plainly be assisted by a report in this case.

It may be that this would be enough and the court would adjourn the case without even hearing from the Prosecution. It may be that the court appears inclined to agree to order a report and so the court asks the Prosecution for a very brief outline of the facts merely to confirm that there is sufficient complexity for the case to warrant the cost of a report.

Asking to sentence without a PSR

The rule is that the court does not tend to pass community penalties unless there is a report from the probation service, which is the body that will administer those penalties in practice. If the Defence is asking for a penalty other than those served in the community, then there would appear to be no need for the report. There are two main occasions when you might consider proceeding to sentence without a PSR:

- The case is *not serious enough* to warrant one. The court has some residual powers to sentence without a PSR. Most notably, the court can sentence the defendant to a fine or to a conditional discharge without a report. If either penalty would (or could) be suitable then it would be worthwhile asking the court to deal with the case without a PSR.

- A custodial sentence is unopposed. If the Defence is quite content to see the defendant given a custodial sentence, and will not seek to persuade the court to sentence the defendant in the community, then the court can pass a custodial sentence without reference to a PSR. The most likely time for this scenario to arise is where the defendant has spent some time in custody already, and would be close to completing a prison sentence. Imagine, for example, that the defendant has been in custody awaiting sentence for two months, and that the tariff for the offence is in the range of four to six months, then the defendant has either served that sentence on remand or is close to having done so. The appropriate application is for the court to sentence the defendant without a report to a term that will lead to release on that day or in the near future.

Making a plea in mitigation

A plea in mitigation is a speech in which the Defence seeks to persuade the court to pass a less serious sentence than it might otherwise have passed. It is not compulsory to make one. It is unlikely, but there may simply be no mitigation in the case and the defendant would be well advised simply to accept a tariff sentence.

Making the plea in mitigation relevant to the sentencing court

The hardest part of a plea in mitigation is ensuring that it remains relevant to the court that is passing sentence. The court may not simply pass a lesser sentence out of sympathy. Too many pleas in mitigation in practice attempt to generate sympathy, but ultimately fail to persuade the court to pass a lesser sentence.

The court has to conduct two assessments of the case before passing sentence:

- First and foremost, it must assess the seriousness of the offence. The primary reference point for any sentence is the seriousness of the offence, and the sentence should reflect that so far as it can.

- The court also looks to secure the rehabilitation of an offender and thereby protect the public from further offending. Therefore, the second assessment that the court will look to conduct is the risk assessment of the offender. This is sometimes called the 'likelihood of re-offending' of the offender.

Unless the plea in mitigation goes to influencing the court on either one of these two assessments it is unlikely to be as effective as it should be.

Take, for example, a defendant who comes from a broken home where they received no support from parents. On a personal level, it may be possible to make the court feel sympathy for the defendant. The better advocate will use a chain of logic to make the point relevant to one of the two assessments that the court is bound to perform. The fact of the broken home will normally lead to some sort of consequence that is relevant to the offence or the offending behaviour. It is understanding this process that will lead to effective advocacy. An example follows below.

Fact	Consequence	Consequence	Consequence	Relevance
D from broken home	D has poor self-esteem	Truanted from school and fell in with bad company	If supported by probation service could learn to choose friends more appropriately	Court could reduce risk to public with a rehabilitation order
As above	D got bored and started taking drugs	Need for money led to offending	D now trying to put drugs behind them (probation offer support)	If drug problem cured, risk to public of re-offending is reduced
As above	As above	As above	D's offence not motivated by malice but by sheer desperation	Offence not as serious as similar offences (motivated by malice)
As above	Little moral guidance given as youth, D rarely considered the consequences of their actions	On this offence, has had to confront the consequences of actions	D remorseful and sees the error of their ways	Now D has a new ability to feel responsible for actions, risk of re-offending has been reduced

In the example above, the fact always leads to the conclusion that the assessment of risk of the offender is reduced or that the offence is not as serious as others in its class. Many advocates outline facts about the offender, but do too little to spell out why and how that fact should actually influence the sentencing court.

The structure of a plea in mitigation

Given that the court will be making the two assessments detailed above, the usual structure employed by defence advocates is to deal with the offence itself (to highlight any features that show that the offence is not so serious) and then with the offender (to show that the defendant is not such a

Advocacy in the Magistrates' Court

risk to the public). Most advocates then conclude by attempting to persuade the court of the advantages of a particular form of sentence. What follows is a more detailed look at each of these component parts.

Reviewing the offence itself

It is helpful to consider that each type of offence has a range of ways in which it can be committed, from the most serious to the least serious. For example, in the case of murder, the 'top end' of the range would be the pre-planned, cold-blooded killing of a person for pure greed, committed in a manner that prolonged the suffering of the victim and cast suspicion and fear upon many other people, and committed by a person enjoying a position of trust with the victim. At the other end of the scale would be the offence born out of the heat of the moment, where there was some degree of provocation (but not enough to be an actual defence), where the violence might not normally have led to the death of the other and where the defendant has shown sincere remorse, etc.

The court generally tries to assess where on this notional scale the instant offence should be put. To that end, it will assess the 'aggravating factors' and the 'mitigating factors' to 'place' the offence in terms of other similar offences.

The defence advocate should extract any mitigating features of the case and emphasise them as much as is possible and seek to persuade the court to view this offence as being as far down the scale of seriousness as possible. It may also be worth pointing out to the court when a particular aggravating feature is absent in a case. For example, the defendant may be charged with robbery. Many robberies are conducted with the use or threat of a weapon. If this is not so in the case that you are dealing with, it would be appropriate to indicate that this is a case free from one of the very serious aggravating factors.

This assessment of the seriousness of the offence in relation to aggravating and mitigating factors is so important and fundamental to sentencing that there are lists of commonly encountered aggravating and mitigating factors. These are reproduced fully and helpfully in *Blackstone's* (2003, Oxford: OUP) and *Archbold* (2002, London: Sweet & Maxwell). There are *specific* factors that relate to *specific* offences: what follows is a list of *general* aggravating and *general* mitigating factors.

In general, aggravating features are:

- planned or premeditated act;
- serious injury;
- high value of goods/property;
- defendant was ringleader of bigger gang;
- weapon used;
- large amount of damage;
- unprovoked;
- drunk;
- breach of trust;
- organised crime;
- young/elderly/vulnerable victim;
- offence committed whilst on bail;
- previous convictions for similar offences;
- offence committed for purely selfish motive.

The following is a list of factors that are generally accepted as mitigating. Think about which ones may be relevant to your particular case and use them in an effective way:

- goods/property of low value;
- few negative consequences of offence on victim;
- offence provoked;
- defendant played minor role;
- spontaneous/impulsive;
- offered compensation to victim;
- shown remorse;

- pleaded guilty;
- co-operated with police and/or admitted guilt immediately;
- no previous convictions;
- offence was out of character/a one-off;
- under severe emotional stress at time;
- in financial difficulties not of own making;
- long time since previous offence;
- led astray by a bad crowd;
- property recovered;
- dependent children/ill spouse, etc;
- secure job/good work record;
- does good work in the community;
- suffered as a result of offence, eg, lost job;
- offence committed out of real need, not to fund extravagant lifestyle;
- offence committed to help another person in need.

Sentencing specimens and offences to be 'taken into consideration' (TICs)

When assessing the seriousness of the offence, it is important to consider whether the offences charged are specimen offences, and whether there are any offences to be taken into consideration.

Specimen offences are charged when it would be too long and laborious to charge every offence said to have been committed separately. This is often the case in charges of deception. If, for example, the defendant is accused of signing on for benefit for work over a three-year period, the Prosecution could either charge an offence for every time the defendant signed up for benefits, or charge the offence twice (once at the start of the period and once at the end of the period). If the court comes to sentence a case where the charges are known to have been specimens and accepted as such, then the Prosecution is perfectly entitled to mention the whole course of conduct and the court will sentence as if there were however many individual offences that make up the whole course of conduct.

Offences to be taken into consideration are different. The police will often ask defendants to admit to offences other than those charged. The bargain that is struck between the police and the defendant is that if the defendant confesses voluntarily to the offence without being charged with it, the police, in return, will promise never to charge the defendant with the offence, but rather simply to mention to the court that the offence has been committed. The court may *not* pass a sentence for the TICs, but the court may use the fact of other offences to count against any attempted mitigation by the Defence. If the defendant is charged with one burglary with another five burglaries on the TIC list, then the court can only sentence for the one burglary, but the court may see the single burglary in the context of offending behaviour and conclude that the single burglary is professional and warrants a serious sentence.

Where a defendant admits offences as TICs, they are asked to sign a list of those offences. A copy is then usually given to the Defence and included in the Crown Prosecution Service (CPS) file. At a convenient moment during the summary of facts, the prosecutor should inform the court that the defendant wishes to have other offences taken into consideration when being sentenced. The District Judge or magistrates will ask the defendant to confirm that the list is correct and that they want the offences to be taken into consideration. The list is not usually read out in full, especially if it is a long one.

Assessing the offender

Most advocates deal with the offender after having assessed the seriousness of the offence. The purpose of giving information about the offender is to indicate why the offence was committed and to suggest how the offender might be dealt with to prevent offences being committed again. See the section above on 'making the plea in mitigation relevant to the sentencing court'.

Any review of the defendant is bound to include a review of any previous convictions and it is important to talk to the defendant about these. Look for any reasons why the current situation is different from the past or how the future might be different from the past. If the defendant has a bad history then the sentence is more likely to be custodial, unless there is something about this juncture in the defendant's life that can credibly indicate that the defendant does not pose a risk to the public of further offending.

Evidence of the defendant's otherwise good character

A plea in mitigation is not confined to a speech from the defence advocate. In many cases the Defence will offer documentary support for points raised on the defendant's behalf, and in some cases the Defence might call a character witness.

So far as documents are concerned, it may be that the defendant can produce a letter from an employer, a reference from a college or school, or a letter from a neighbour or other responsible person. Sometimes defendants like to write a letter of remorse for the court to read and it is perfectly acceptable to pass this up. Check all documents carefully first. Some defendants look to submit bogus job offers or other documents that appear to be forgeries. It is a matter of discretion which documents, if any, should support your plea in mitigation.

If there is a person who could speak particularly strongly or credibly on the defendant's behalf, the advocate should consider calling them as a witness. Be careful to reserve this for cases where the impact of the witness is likely to far exceed any representation that you could make. Examples might include calling someone ordained by the church or any other religious person who can give evidence of good works done by the defendant. With some young defendants it can be beneficial to call a parent or other adult to give evidence of any new maturity or change in character. The armed services often send a superior officer to court when someone in their service is convicted of an offence. It can often be very helpful for a court to hear from this person about the defendant's character and career background.

It is rare, but sometimes the author of the PSR attends court. If this is the case and if the probation officer seems particularly well disposed to the defendant, it can be helpful to call the probation officer to expand upon any matters dealt with in the report and to allow the probation officer to express orally why they seem so well disposed to the defendant.

You can also call the defendant. In practice this is the most rare of all courses to take. If you consider that the defendant can express something more powerfully than you can, then consider calling them as a witness. Beware: the defendant might be very expressive in conference but much more wooden and less convincing when addressing the court. You can also never be sure what they might say. Generally *do not risk* calling the defendant but simply remember that you may do so if you think that there is a compelling reason why it might be beneficial.

Recommending a particular form of sentence

Most advocates would conclude a plea in mitigation with an invitation to the court to consider a particular form of sentence. Best practice is to do so very courteously and to avoid being too direct. It would be better to *avoid* a submission such as:

> This is not a serious offence and it should be dealt with by a fine.

Instead, it would be better to say:

> The court may take the view there are many cases more serious than this, and I ask the court to consider whether a fine may not be sufficient punishment in the case.

When addressing the court on the appropriate sentence, the emphasis should be on *asking* the court, or *suggesting* something to the court, rather than *telling* the court.

Be realistic in your proposals. Do not aggravate the court by asking for a sentence which clearly falls short of the court's public duty to pass a sentence commensurate to the seriousness of the offence.

There is often more than one form of sentence that would fit the offence. If this is the case, the best course to adopt is to highlight the advantages of one over the other. It can help to weigh both of them up and seek to persuade the court that there is more merit in one than the other. This is especially so when the case is on the borderline between a custodial and a non-custodial sentence. You might consider a submission such as:

> Sir, I accept of course that the court will be considering a custodial sentence. That would mark the seriousness of the case. In my submission, such a sentence would not address the problems that this young man/woman has been facing and would be unlikely to address the reason for his/her offending. For that reason I ask the court to consider passing a Rehabilitation Order. The order would address the particular needs of this defendant as set out in the PSR. Given that the defendant is a relatively young man/woman and that his/her record is not a bad one, the court may think that he/she still has some hope of being properly rehabilitated in the community and I urge the court to pass a sentence to assist in this process ...

If the PSR recommends a sentence that concurs with your analysis of what would constitute a good sentence in the case, make sure that you make it plain to the court that you are arguing for the same disposal as the probation service.

If the PSR recommends a sentence that does *not* concur with your instructions or analysis, you will need to explain carefully to the court why it should follow your proposal for sentence rather than that suggested in the report.

Checklist for making a plea in mitigation

- Have a structure in mind, rather than saying things as you think of them. For example, you may want to deal first with the offence itself, then with the defendant's personal circumstances and finally with the type of sentence which should be imposed. Prepare your speech as much as possible, even if this means scribbling something down on the day, while you are waiting to be called on.

- Having discussed the possible sentences with the defendant, ascertain what type of sentence would be the most desirable and focus your plea accordingly. If the defendant agrees with the recommendation in the PSR, then ask the court to follow the recommendation and explain why that type of sentence would be most appropriate.

- If there is a PSR, make sure that the court has had a chance to look at it before you mitigate. Do not read it all out, but refer to any paragraphs which you feel are important and read out any sentences that are particularly helpful.

- Highlight and emphasise any mitigating factors (see above). Make any mitigating factors relevant to the court's assessment of the seriousness of the offence and/or the likelihood of the defendant offending again.

- Be aware of aggravating features and try to disassociate the defendant from them. However, you should be realistic and where there are aggravating features it is generally better to acknowledge them, but to say that there are strong mitigating factors that ought to be considered.

- Do not make your speech too long. Use pace and pauses to gain maximum effect. Give the court time to take notes of what you are saying, especially when giving details of the defendant's financial circumstances.

- You can call character witnesses, although this is rarely done. However, you may well have letters about the defendant's character, work situation or any medical condition and, at an appropriate point in your speech, you should hand the letter up to the judge or magistrates, explaining what it is.

- It may not be appropriate to say that the defendant expresses remorse, when the sentence follows a trial throughout which the defendant has professed their innocence!

- Where the defendant is at risk of a custodial sentence, emphasise any responsibilities which they may have and the consequences of imprisonment, eg, likely to lose employment. If the defendant suffers from drug or alcohol abuse, suggest that a sentence that will facilitate help with the addiction will be far more beneficial than prison.

- Be realistic. Do not suggest to the court, unless there really are exceptional circumstances, that a prison sentence is not appropriate where the sentencing guidelines clearly show otherwise.

- If the defendant pleaded guilty, ask for credit to be given for their guilty plea.

- It is very rare to refer to any authorities when mitigating. However, if you do refer to any law, have copies of it for the prosecutor, the clerk/legal adviser, the magistrates or the judge. Give a full citation so that the relevant section can be found.

Prosecutor's role

At a sentencing hearing the prosecutor should deal with the following:

- *A summary of the facts of the case*
  You can base it on the 'Summary of Evidence' in the CPS file. It is important to check this for accuracy if there is time to do so. If the Defence informs you that it disputes

your version of events, you may be able to reach an agreed version, or you may have to ask for a Newton hearing (see Chapter 10). When addressing the court, prosecutors should adopt a *neutral attitude* and not attempt to influence the court with regard to sentence. Keep to the main facts and, where appropriate, include details of the way the offence was committed, any aggravating or mitigating features, any injuries, the value of any loss, details of arrest, the defendant's explanation at interview and whether the defendant co-operated with police or pleaded guilty. Where the sentencing takes place immediately following a trial there is no need to outline the facts again as they will be fresh in the minds of the court.

• *Evidence of character and antecedents*
Having dealt with the facts, pass up any previous convictions of the defendant. Confirm with the defence advocate that the list of previous convictions is correct and say to the court that the list is an agreed list. The convictions need to be spelt out in open court (for the benefit of those attending who do not have sight of a copy). Where there is a long list, it may be worth omitting the older convictions or summarising them. Explain what you are intending to do, eg:

> Perhaps it would assist the court if I started at 1995?

Anything over 10 years old is often thought to be of little relevance, but be prepared to be guided by the court. With the rest of the convictions, tell the court where and when the conviction was, what it was for and what the sentence was, eg:

> On 5 September 1998 Mr Ball was convicted at Southwark Crown Court for burglary, for which he received a sentence of one year's imprisonment.

• *Ask for costs*

See below.

Prosecution costs

Where a defendant is convicted of an offence, the court can order them to pay to the Prosecution such costs as it considers just and reasonable. The amount must be specified by the court and cannot be assessed at a later date. For example, when outlining the facts of the case to the magistrates after a plea of guilty, the prosecutor will usually end by saying that there is an application for Prosecution costs in the sum of, say £90. Prosecutors should make sure that they have the relevant figures available. The defence advocate will then put forward the defendant's mitigation, highlighting their financial circumstances, so that the court can assess whether the defendant should pay all or any of the costs asked for by the Prosecution.

The court will assess what, in its opinion, it is just and reasonable for the defendant to pay. For example, if a defendant has been convicted of some offences but acquitted of others, the court may award the Prosecution part of its total costs.

Before making an order for costs against a defendant, the court must be satisfied that they have the means and ability to pay, although the amount of costs ordered may take the defendant up to a year, or possibly more, to pay.

If the defendant is ordered to pay a fine, the costs awarded should bear some relationship to the level of the fine (*R v Jones* (1988) unreported). The court should not reduce a fine to accommodate an order for costs. If the court orders payment of a fine or compensation not exceeding £5, it cannot order the defendant to pay the Prosecution costs unless, in the particular circumstances of the case, it considers it right to do so.

Where a juvenile is convicted in a youth court, any order for costs cannot exceed the amount of any fine that is properly imposed on them, unless their parents are ordered to pay the fine. Where the defendant is given an immediate custodial sentence, it is unusual to impose an order for costs as they will have no income out of which to make payments.

If, however, there is good reason to suppose that a defendant has substantial capital assets, eg, from the proceeds of crime, an order for costs may be made.

If the prosecutor is a private prosecutor the court may, if the offence is indictable (or is criminal damage of under £5,000), order the prosecutor's costs to be paid out of central funds. The court can do this even when the Prosecution is unsuccessful. The court may assess the amount to be paid out of central funds at the hearing if the prosecutor agrees, or the clerk may assess the amount at a later date. There is no similar power to award the costs of the CPS or any other public authority out of central funds, even if the Prosecution is successful.

Checklist of sentences available to the court

This is a potentially huge subject, and there have been many legislative changes. This should not be viewed as a primary source but as a quick reference guide:

- *Custodial sentences*
  No custodial sentence can be passed unless the offence (or combination of offences) is/are so serious that *only* a custodial sentence can be justified. Remember that for all sentences under three years, the defendant will be released after serving half the sentence – provided they have been of good behaviour. Any time spent in custody on remand *does* count towards the sentence served.

- *Detention in a young offenders' institution*
  This is a custodial sentence for those aged 18 to 20 inclusive. The relevant age is the age on conviction. Defendant must be represented before this order can be passed. Maximum terms are the same as for adults. Much the same as a custodial sentence for adults except the actual institution is aimed at this age group.

- *Detention and Training Order (DTO)*
  This is a period of detention at a young offenders' institution followed by supervision on release. The

sentence is available for those aged 15–17 inclusive if 'only a custodial sentence is justified'. For those aged 12–14 inclusive, *add* the requirement that the young offender is a 'persistent offender', and for those under 12 years of age, the requirement is that '*only* a period of detention would protect the public from harm' from that person. Periods of time in custody on remand are *not* automatically removed from the order. The period of the DTO should take account of any time in custody on remand. The order runs in two parts (detention followed by training/supervision) and so the order must be for one of the following number of months: four, six, eight, 10, 12, 18 or 24.

- *Suspended sentences*
  This is a custodial sentence, which is not immediate, but suspended for between one and two years. The court can only suspend the sentence if there are 'exceptional circumstances' in the case. You can combine suspended sentences with fines but not a community sentence or custody. Good character, youth and a guilty plea are not exceptional circumstances. A further offence during the period of the suspension will normally lead to the sentence being activated, and passed as a consecutive sentence.

- *Suspended sentence supervision order*
  This is a suspended sentence of more than six months with the additional requirement that the defendant be monitored by a probation order for any amount of the period of the suspension.

- *Community punishment order (CPO)*
  This is the replacement for community service. A CPO consists of unpaid work in the community (collecting litter, painting, etc). This sentence cannot be passed unless the offence is 'serious enough' to warrant such a sentence. The offence must be imprisonable. The defendant must be aged 16 or over. The CPO must be for between 40 and 240 hours and should be completed in 12 months.

Sentencing

- *Community rehabilitation order (CRO)*
  This is the replacement for the old probation order. It is a sentence involving a probation officer supervising the defendant and requiring the defendant to attend meetings with the probation officer to look at the defendant's behaviour and attitude to offending. The defendant must be aged 16 or over. The CRO must be for six months or more but less than three years. Provided that the limits are defined, the CRO can include 'additional requirements' to secure the defendant's rehabilitation: these might include a requirement on the place of residence, a requirement to attend activities (up to 60 days), to attend probation centres, and, most importantly, to submit to treatment for an alcohol or drug dependency.

- *Community punishment and rehabilitation order*
  This is an order with a CPO component and a CRO component. These were formerly called (and are occasionally still referred to as) combination orders. The defendant must be aged 16 or over. The CPO component must be for between 40 and 100 hours and the CRO component must last for between 12 months and three years. The conditions required for either type of component sentence also attach to this sentence.

- *Curfew order*
  This order requires a person to remain at a specified location at specified times of the day (although in reality this means during the night time). The order can specify different locations for different days. The order cannot be for less than two hours per day, nor for more than 12 hours. The order can last for up to six months for adults, and up to three months for those under 16. The order may be combined with other orders (except custody or conditional or absolute discharge).

- *Supervision order (SO)*
  This is effectively the youth court version of a CRO for those under 18. For those who are aged 16 or 17, the court

Advocacy in the Magistrates' Court

could order either sentence. The purpose of the two orders really lies in the desire to have a specialist programme for the younger offenders. With those aged 16 or 17, if the offending behaviour is more often seen in adult offenders then the CRO is the more suitable sentence (as it will be administered by the probation service). Where the 'problem' is one more usually associated with young offenders then the better order would be an SO (administered by a member of the youth justice team).

- *Attendance centre order*
  This order requires those aged under 21 to attend an attendance centre at given times and accept instruction and supervision once there. There is a general minimum number of hours of 12. If the defendant is under 14 this may be reduced if 12 hours appears excessive to the court given the young age of the defendant. 12 hours is also the normal limit, but can be exceeded if the court considers that 12 hours is insufficient, subject to the absolute maximums of 24 hours for those under 16, and 36 hours for those aged 16 or over but under 21.

- *Drug treatment and testing order (DTTO)*
  This is a community order available to those aged 16 or over. It is a rehabilitative order dealing particularly with drug dependency. The order must last for between six months and three years, and requires the defendant to submit to treatment. Much the same order could be given under a CRO with an 'additional condition' to have drug treatment, but there are several differences in when the order is given and how it is monitored. An additional requirement on a CRO requires the dependency to have caused the offence (or contributed to it). Under a DTTO, first, no causal link between dependency and offence needs to be proved. Secondly, the DTTO is only available for drug dependency, not alcohol, gambling, solvent abuse, etc. Thirdly, the DTTO includes testing the defendant for drugs. The CRO does not carry any

compulsory testing. Because of the testing element, the defendant must express a willingness to be placed on a DTTO before the sentence can be passed. Finally, there is a requirement under a DTTO that the defendant's progress be monitored and reviewed by the court that made the order, not less than every month. The first review must be a full review in court. If good progress is being made, subsequent reviews can be more administrative. If progress is unsatisfactory, the court can explore an amendment to the order, a further review, or revocation and re-sentence of the order.

- *Action plan order*
  This sentence is available for juveniles under the age of 18. The order runs for three months. The idea is that the court places the defendant under the supervision of a 'responsible officer' (a probation officer or a social worker) who works with the defendant to implement a plan of action to secure their rehabilitation or prevent the commission of further offences by the defendant. The court may order a review of the progress of the action plan, such review being within 21 days of the start of the order. Amendments can be made to the order at this review.

- *Exclusion order*
  This order is not yet in force, but when it is, it will allow courts to exclude the defendant for a period of up to a year from any place. The order will be able to specify different places and different days if appropriate.

- *Reparation order*
  This is available for those under 18 years of age. The order requires the defendant to make reparation (in the form of unpaid labour) to the victim of an offence, or any other person affected by the offence. The number of hours of work is limited to 24 in aggregate. This is not a community penalty and does not need to pass the 'serious enough' test.

- *Absolute discharge*
  This is a sentence of no penalty. The defendant is still a convicted person, but there is no penalty for the offence.

A conditional discharge is in effect a deterrent sentence, in that no penalty is passed, but the court reserves the right to sentence the defendant on any future date if they commit any further offences during the period of the discharge. The period of the discharge can be between six months and three years. No other punitive penalty can be passed alongside a conditional discharge. There are no age limits for discharges.

- *Parenting order*

  This is available for a parent or guardian of any child or young person who falls to be sentenced for an offence. The order specifies various requirements to be complied with for 12 months, and a period of counselling or guidance for up to three months (for up to once a week). The requirements include such instruction as ensuring the child or young person is accompanied to school, or making sure they are indoors by a certain hour in the evening, etc. If the child or young person being sentenced is under 16 years of age, the court should pass such an order unless it finds that it is not in the interests of preventing the commission of offences by the child or young person to pass such an order. If this is the view of the court, it must state as much in court.

- *Parental bind over*

  A parental bind over draws a parent or guardian into a recognisance with the court that the parent or guardian will take proper control of the child or young person in their care. If the recognisance is breached, the parent or guardian stands to lose the sum of money specified in the order (no more than £1,000). The order applies when the child or young person concerned is under 16 years of age. The court should make an order binding the parent or guardian over, unless it finds that it is not in the interests of preventing the commission of offences by the child or young person to pass such an order. If this is the view of the court, it must state as much in court.

- *Fines*

  The court can fine any defendant – the limit normally being set down by the statute creating the offence. The limit is very seldom reached since the court is obliged to consider the defendant's ability to pay any fine when setting the tariff. The court must give any defendant a reasonable amount of time to pay any fine. A fine is often paid in instalments. The defence advocate should be ready to tell the court about the defendant's financial circumstances, and to offer a figure for an instalment payment of any fine. The court can review fines, and the rate of payment, if the defendant's circumstances change. Ultimately, the defendant can be sentenced to serve a 'period in default' of paying the fine. This period should be specified when the original fine is passed down and is on a standard scale.

- *Compensation*

  Compensation should be considered in every case where there is any personal injury, loss or damage suffered by the complainant in a case for which the defendant stands convicted. There need not be a formal application before the court for the court to grant compensation. The amount of any order, and the rate of payment, must take into account the defendant's ability to pay. Compensation should not be an alternative to sentence. It can be ordered alongside almost all other forms of sentence (but generally not custody). Where there is a fine and compensation, the court will collect and pass on the compensation first.

- *Forfeiture and restitution*

  The courts have the power to order the forfeiture (and destruction) of illegally held goods (eg, guns and drugs) and to order goods to be returned to their lawful owner if that person has been identified.

16   Breach proceedings

What are breach proceedings?

The phrase 'breach proceedings' denotes proceedings brought by the probation service against a defendant who is currently subject to a community sentence. The proceedings are brought on account of an alleged failure by the defendant to comply with the terms of the order.

The person against whom the proceedings are brought is a convicted person serving a sentence, and the probation service tends to refer to convicted people as the 'offender' rather than the 'defendant'. This chapter will include the term 'offender' accordingly.

What constitutes a breach?

The usual complaint made against an offender is their attendance record. You may hear the expression 'national minimum standards', which is a code for the probation service to define what can properly be expected from offenders in terms of compliance with any order administered by the probation service.

The probation service does not expect every convicted person to attend every session perfectly on time, and the offender will not be 'breached' for attending five minutes late for one appointment on one occasion. How many chances the offender is given is a matter of some discretion, and will take account of any reasons given by the offender for the problems of attendance.

It is not only attendance that is the subject of a potential breach. There could be problems with attitude and commitment to community rehabilitation or problems with the quality of work on community punishment.

As a rule of thumb if an offender misses two sessions without adequate reason then the service may issue proceedings. If there are problems with three appointments there is bound to be an action for the breach.

How are proceedings brought?

Proceedings are brought by the probation service itself and are not passed on to the Crown Prosecution Service (CPS). Many barristers will pick up work prosecuting breaches on behalf of the probation service at some point in their practice.

The proceedings are usually initiated by summons, although there could be an application for a warrant for the offender's arrest.

Breaching a sentence is not a criminal offence. The proceedings that follow involve the offender being asked to admit or deny the breach, and indeed the passing of sentence, but these are not ordinary criminal proceedings following the commission of a crime.

The probation officer who is nominally in charge of administering the offender's sentence will write a report into how and why it is said that a breach of the order has occurred. The statement will normally describe how the offender was notified of their commitments to the order and the expectations and requirements that will be made of them. They will have signed a form indicating that they understand these requirements. The procedure is then that the service will write letters to the offender advising of when and where to attend for subsequent appointments. The statement will describe the problems that have been encountered in administering the order.

Having a conference in a breach case

The 'defence' available to the complaint is that there is a 'reasonable excuse' for the problems with the order. It is rare that the offender will actually take issue with the *fact* that appointments were missed or that they were late, etc. It is almost invariably the case that the issue is actually one of whether there are *reasonable explanations* for the behaviour.

The sort of defence that you will hear is that the offender found themselves without any money for transport to get to an appointment, or that the letter of instruction went missing in the post.

The defence advocate will need to ask the offender whether they accept the breach of the order or whether they wish to argue 'reasonable excuse'. If the breach is accepted then you will need to take instructions on whether there is any chance of the order working in the future. Also you must take instructions on the original offence and all matters of mitigation, since you may have to perform a full plea in mitigation; see the sections below on punishment for breach and be careful to address the issue of whether the breach was 'wilful and persistent' (see below).

The offender may be reluctant to accept a breach, but the excuses for the behaviour complained of seem to be rather weak. You will simply need to advise on whether the magistrates are likely to accept the excuses as being reasonable. Arguing that the appointment time was inconvenient to an offender is unlikely to be sufficient. The probation service itself is well aware of the problems and weaknesses faced by many of the people with community sentences. The courts usually view the probation service as being reasonable, and you can normally guarantee that if the excuse was not good enough for probation then it will not persuade the court either.

There will be cases where you are instructed to deny the breach. If this is the case you need to consider whether you need to have the relevant probation officer in court to answer any question that you may want to put. If it is really a matter of the offender explaining the difficulties with transport or money, etc, then you can have a short hearing without having to call witnesses other than just the offender.

At court

As these are not proceedings leading to trial, the rules on disclosure, etc, do not strictly apply. The prosecutor will *not* usually be the same person as the CPS prosecutor so you should not have much difficulty finding the person bringing the proceedings and they should be able to explain the substance of the complaint. What follows is the procedure adopted once in court.

Summary of procedure for establishing whether there is a breach

1 The clerk of the court/legal adviser will put the information to the offender that they have breached the order for order X imposed at Y magistrates' court.

2 The offender will accept or deny the breach.

3 If the breach is accepted the case will proceed to punishment for the breach and possible re-sentence for the original offence. (See below.)

4 If the breach is denied the court will need to decide when to hear the issue of the breach. The Defence will need to inform the court how many witnesses will be needed to establish the denial.

5 The court will either adjourn to secure witness attendance or hear the matter there and then.

6 The hearing is not subject to the normal rules of evidence.

7 If the probation officer is to give evidence, they will be examined-in-chief by the representative of the probation service and then cross-examined by the Defence. If the probation officer's evidence is not disputed, the statement prepared by them will simply be read out.

8 The offender will need to give evidence to establish the reasonable excuse (or to deny the fact of the breach at all in those rare circumstances). They will be examined-in-chief and then cross-examined.

9 The Defence could make a submission at the end of the evidence to seek to persuade the court that the excuse is sufficient to find that there has been no breach. If the hearing has been short then the Defence should not repeat the evidence and point out the very obvious.

10 The bench will then decide whether the breach is proved to its satisfaction. If there is no breach then that is the end of the matter. Otherwise the breach will need to be punished. (See below.)

Punishing the breach without re-sentencing the original offence

The first question is whether a further pre-sentence report is required. It seems odd that the probation service brings proceedings against the offender, and then the case is adjourned for the same people to write a report as to how the offender should be punished for the breach. In general terms, if the offender wishes to remain out of custody it will help to show that they can recommit to the order and to say so in a further report. An adjournment for the preparation of a report will give the offender valuable time to make amends and establish new commitment to the sentence. It is routinely the case that the order breaks down at the time of the complaint, but is operative again by the time the case comes to court.

It might be assumed that once the order is proven to be breached then the original order is bound to be revoked and the offender re-sentenced for the original offence. This is not correct. Indeed, if the original sentencing court thought that the case did not merit custody originally, then there is an emphasis on attempting to deal with the breach *without* resorting to custody. Only in cases where the breach is 'wilful and persistent' can a community sentence be revoked and replaced with a custodial sentence (see below).

Therefore, a breach *can* attract a separate penalty, which is imposed *without* revoking the order. That penalty can be a fine of up to £1,000 or community punishment. The total number of hours of community punishment must not exceed 100 for the breach alone, or 240 for the combination of the original sentence and the punishment for the breach. If the original sentence involved community rehabilitation and community punishment the total number of hours for the original sentence and the breach must not exceed 100.

Revoking the original sentence and re-sentencing

When the original sentence was passed the court must have come to the view that a custodial sentence was not the correct sentence. This could be arrived at in two ways. The court might have concluded that a custodial sentence could be justified, but not *only* a custodial sentence could be justified – one could justify a community penalty too. If the court did not make any such comment, the original sentencing court *must* have found that the offence was *not* so serious that only a custodial penalty could be justified (ie, the offence did not pass the 'custody threshold').

The relevance of this is that once a court has accepted that a case falls below the custody threshold then it can *only* pass a custodial sentence following a breach if the breach is 'wilful and persistent' (Sched 3, para 4 of the Powers of the Criminal Courts (Sentencing) Act 2000).

There is no definition of 'wilful and persistent', but it must surely indicate something more than an 'average' breach, or else the phrase would be redundant. What turns a 'run of the mill' breach into a wilful and persistent breach is unclear, but it must describe a situation towards the more extreme end of the range, where the offender has made very little effort whatever and where the difficulties in attending have derived almost entirely from the offender's poor attitude.

In any submission concerning whether the courts should revoke the order and re-sentence, it would be appropriate to comment upon the nature of the breach. If there were nothing out of the ordinary about the breach, you would be entitled to submit that custody *is not an option* to the court since the breach itself is not 'wilful and persistent'.

If custody is not an option open to the court for the reasons set out above, it would hardly seem necessary to revoke and re-sentence since the offender seems bound to be given a further attempt to complete some form of community order.

It may be that the original sentence was badly conceived (but be careful how you put this). Alternatively, the order may have become unworkable for some good reason that could not have been originally conceived. For example, it may be that the sentencing court thought that the offender would benefit from some support from the probation service, and the court consequently passed a community rehabilitation order. In reality, the offender needed little help and put their life together before the order really got far underway. The order then collapses because the offender sees no point in attending the sessions as they seem hardly relevant. They are charged with a breach because they do not attend appointments. In this example it may be worth re-sentencing simply to pass a better or more relevant sentence. These situations are rare. If the offender has made really good progress, the service itself can apply to revoke the order, as it is no longer necessary to enforce it.

In any case where there is the prospect of revoking the original sentence and re-sentencing, the courts should take into account the amount of the sentence that has already been completed. If, for example, the offender had completed 150 hours out of 180, the new sentence would be totally different than if they had completed only 10 hours. If there has been substantial performance of the order it may be that a fine would take care of the breach *and* the remainder of the original sentence.

The procedure for re-sentence is just like the original sentencing. There will be an opening of the facts from the prosecutor. Remember that the person prosecuting the case will be instructed by the probation service and not by the CPS. The practical effect of this is that the communication between the CPS and the probation service is not always very good and the probation prosecutor may have scant information about the original offence. It is routinely the case that the defence advocate knows a great deal more about the original offence than the person supposed to present the facts to the court.

The plea in mitigation for the re-sentence will be almost identical to the original plea, but with the addition of commentary about the amount of the order performed and the character of the breach.

Summary of the procedure for re-sentencing

1   Once there is an admission or a finding of a breach, the bench or clerk/legal adviser will ask whether the probation service is looking to have the order revoked and the offender re-sentenced for the original offence. The court will also ask the Defence if there is an application for a further probation service report (PSR).

2   If the breach is minor and the probation service is *not* seeking a revocation and re-sentence, the Defence might ask that the case be dealt with there and then by the imposition of a fine.

3   If the breach is more serious and the probation service recommends revoking the original sentence, then the case will usually be adjourned for a PSR. The Defence may have a proposal for how to deal with the case that would not necessitate adjourning for a PSR. In the case of an adjournment the issue of bail will need to be addressed.

4   When penalising a breach alone, the prosecutor will describe the breach, and the Defence can offer an apology for the breach and express the offender's commitment to continuing the order. The Defence will normally outline the offender's ability to pay a fine.

5   If there is an application to revoke the original order and re-sentence, the prosecutor will outline the facts of the original offence and formally apply to the court for the original sentence to be revoked.

6   The Defence can then make a plea in mitigation and make submissions on whether the breach was 'wilful and persistent' and on what the court should do in terms of the original order and punishment for the breach.

7   The bench will then announce its decision, which may involve revocation of the original order and a re-sentence, or it may simply involve a penalty for the breach. The court is quite entitled to pass a community penalty even though the probation service has asked for the order to be revoked.

17 Road traffic hearings

Introduction

One cannot practise in criminal law in the magistrates' court and avoid dealing with road traffic cases. This chapter looks at the scenarios that occur most regularly in practice in cases that might attract public funding.

Most offences are summary only and this may lull the advocate into a false sense that these will be simple matters. In fact, they are sometimes complex and involved. People care passionately about their cars and clients can be more anxious about road traffic penalties than some of the 'conventional' criminal penalties.

A further pressure is created by the tendency of many magistrates' courts to list all the road traffic cases together with the result that upwards of 50 cases might be listed in one court on one day.

Getting a representation order

Defendants are often unrepresented in court because the primary criterion for the granting of a representation order (RO) is the likelihood of loss of liberty, and few driving offences carry this penalty. However, in the case of more serious offences such as drink-driving or disqualified driving the offender *may* be at risk of custody and an RO should be sought.

The other headings in the RO application form (Form A) may also be relevant. Many defendants facing a disqualification will potentially be facing a loss of livelihood from being unable to drive to work. This will provide strong grounds for seeking an RO. You will need to know the state of the defendant's licence and the penalties available for the offences before you can assess whether the defendant is at risk of a ban. The penalties are listed in Appendix 5.

For further guidance on filling out Form A, please see Chapter 4.

If the offence arises from a road traffic accident, the parties' insurers may provide funding.

The notice of intended prosecution

In almost any motoring case, a person who is suspected of committing an offence must be put on notice that a prosecution may follow as a consequence of the driving complained of. This is a statutory requirement under ss 1 and 2 of the Road Traffic Offenders Act 1988.

If an officer is at a scene and speaks to a driver about their driving, the officer must give an oral warning which is plain and that the defendant has understood. If the offence is recorded without any face to face contact (eg, a speed camera) then the Prosecution has to send a formal 'notice of intended prosecution' within 14 days.

The reason for this requirement is that a defendant may be wholly unaware that they could be asked to defend their driving in a court of law on some date in the future. If they are put on notice that they may have to do this then at least a defendant can take steps to try to remember the driving in question so that they might adequately argue their case.

Failure to give this notice would seem to be fatal to any proceedings.

The warning is deemed to have been given unless the defendant can show on the balance of probabilities that it was not.

Consider getting a plan or photographs

In some cases, especially where there has been an accident, a plan of the scene speaks a thousand words. Consider carefully whether a plan would be helpful to explain the case to the magistrates.

The plan should be taken in two stages. First, you need to make sure that you understand the defendant's case, so draw a plan in conference and let the defendant draw all over it so that you can understand what their account is. This should not make any appearance in court!

Best practice is then to draw another plan for the court that is the plan of the road *only*. Go and see the prosecutor and try to get the prosecutor to agree the document and then it can be used as an exhibit. The defendant can then mark on the plan where they say they were at a given point, as part of the evidence. The defendant will be on oath and so each marking they make on the plan can be a part of their sworn evidence.

In an ideal world, having agreed the basic layout of the road, you should copy the plan so that each witness can mark a plan of their own in the witness box. The court will then have a set of plans to reflect the account of each of the witnesses. You will have to ask the prosecutor or even the usher or legal adviser to see if anyone has access to a copier. If you have had a chance to do one before you set out for court then so much the better.

Witnesses always find it easier to demonstrate than to explain in clear terms what the vehicles were doing at any given time. If you have conduct of the case prior to it coming to court, then you should obtain photographs depicting not only the area but also the field of view of the parties involved.

Individual offences

Drink-driving

The offence

There are at least 10 varieties of the offence under ss 4 and 5 of the Road Traffic Act 1988. They cover driving or being in charge or attempting to drive whilst being unfit or over the prescribed level. The important distinctions are between: (1) being in charge as opposed to actually driving; and (2) being unfit as opposed to being over the limit.

'Being in charge' of a vehicle is something more than just owning the vehicle and something less than driving it. If someone walks out of a pub to find their car and the keys are in their hand, they are 'in charge' of the vehicle. Once the Prosecution has raised evidence of the defendant being in charge, to avoid conviction it is for the Defence to argue that there is insufficient evidence to establish 'control', or for the defendant to show on the balance of probabilities that they were not actually going to drive.

'Driving' is self-explanatory. Normally there will be evidence of the defendant being seen actually driving, although weak evidence of the defendant being the driver can be supported by circumstantial evidence such as possession of keys to the car, the bonnet being warm, the defendant hiding, etc.

'Being over the limit' is a matter of scientific proof and of formal procedure which is outlined below. 'Being unfit' is normally a matter of expert opinion offered by a police doctor. To show that someone was unfit there will normally be evidence of: (1) poor driving; and (2) the physical state of the defendant. This *may* be enough to show that the defendant was unfit to drive through drink or drugs. It is much safer and better for the police to have the defendant seen in custody by a doctor who can give an opinion to the level of intoxication and the likely effect on the driving. *Lay* opinion on the effect of alcohol or drugs on driving is not admissible.

The police can carry out a roadside breath test if: (1) they reasonably suspect an individual to have alcohol in their body; *or* (2) they reasonably suspect the driver of having committed a traffic offence; *or* (3) there has been an accident. This test will not give a reading but merely an indication of the presence of alcohol. A positive indication will lead to an arrest and further testing. However, failing to provide a breath sample without good cause when requested will also lead to prosecution. See below.

Where the roadside test indicates the presence of alcohol this will be followed up at the police station. The procedure at the station is recorded in a booklet labelled MG/DD/A. This will record information provided by the offender in relation to pre-arrest and post-arrest consumption of alcohol, food, medication and cigarettes.

It will also record brief details of the reason for requiring a breath sample and notes on the nature and demeanour of the defendant at the time of arrest. When the station procedure is completed the machine will provide the police with a 'till receipt' showing the level of alcohol in the breath.

It is always important to check the calibration cycle recorded on the till receipt. This should be between 32 and 38µg. If the result of the calibration is outside these parameters the breath test will be void. The till receipt must be attached to the inside cover of the MG/DD/A form.

Statutory levels
The prescribed limits of alcohol in blood, breath and urine are: blood 80µg in 100ml; breath 35µg in 100ml; and urine 107µg in 100ml.

Where the result of the breath test is between 35 and 39µg the police have discretion whether to prosecute.

Where the reading of alcohol in the breath is under 50µg then the police must offer the defendant the statutory option of taking a blood test. Often it will take some time for a doctor to attend to take the sample by which time the level of alcohol in the body may have dropped further. Where a blood sample has been taken either as a statutory option or because the offender has a justifiable ground for not providing a breath sample, then this information will be recorded in MG/DD/B.

The sample will be split into two and the police will send their sample for testing. Whenever this is done there should be a trail of statements that show: (1) how the sample was labelled; (2) where it was stored; (3) when and where it was sent for testing. These are called statements of continuity. It is always important to ensure that the sample that was taken is the sample that was tested. Many prosecutions break down because the continuity cannot be shown. The same must always be done for urine samples.

Expert evidence

Expert evidence will also be useful in cases where the defendant is alleging either the spiking of drinks or consumption of alcohol *after* the driving. Experts are able to provide 'back calculations' which attempt to remove theoretically the alcohol said to be consumed after the driving, to determine what the true level of alcohol *would have been* at the time when the defendant was driving the car. As mentioned above, obtaining expert reports may take some time and the report will need to be served on the Prosecution in advance of the hearing. Likewise, expert reports are needed if the Defence is trying to establish justifiable reasons for a defendant to have refused to provide a sample by any of the means stated above.

Penalties

Any offence of *driving* with excess alcohol or being unfit through drink and drugs will attract a ban of at least 12 months. The length increases with the levels of alcohol concerned. Where the defendant has been convicted of drink-driving in the 10 years preceding the current offence, then there is a compulsory minimum disqualification of three years. In more serious cases where the level of alcohol in the breath is over 100 then the courts begin to consider custody. The maximum term is six months.

If the charge relates to being *'in charge'*, disqualification is discretionary but endorsement of the licence with 10 points is obligatory. A prison sentence can be passed of up to three months.

In determining the length of any ban, the court will have regard to the amount of alcohol consumed and the nature of the driving at the time of the offence. The ban itself is not regarded as a penalty and the court will also impose some other form of sentence ranging from fines to custody.

A disqualification can however be avoided if there are: (1) 'special reasons'; or (2) the defendant can argue 'exceptional hardship'. These will be discussed in greater detail below.

Both the defendant and the court should be reminded by the defence advocate that drink-driving awareness rehabilitation courses are available. The court can indicate that if such a course is completed the offender can receive a reduction in the ban of up to 25% of the total length. This course has to be funded by the offender; the fees in 2003 are in the region of £150. Ask the court to take this into account if it is considering a financial penalty.

If an offender is convicted of a second drink-driving offence within 10 years, on application to the DVLA (Driver and Vehicle Licensing Agency) for the return of the licence at the end of the period of disqualification, they may be required to undergo a medical assessment.

Further, it should be noted that a disqualified driver can apply for the early revocation of the ban. No application is to be made for the removal of the disqualification before the expiration of whichever is relevant of the following periods:

- two years, if the disqualification is for less than four years; or

- one-half of the period of disqualification if it is for less than 10 years but not less than four years; or

- five years in any other case.

The court should also have regard to the character of the person disqualified, the nature of the original offence and any other circumstances of the case. It is not unusual for the police to have been contacted and asked for their opinion on the matter.

Failure to provide a specimen (s 7 of the Road Traffic Act 1988)
If the defendant refuses to give a specimen of breath or blood then the charge of drink-driving will normally be abandoned and the charge of failing to provide a specimen will be

preferred in its place. The failure may occur at the roadside or back at the police station.

At the roadside it would be an available defence to argue that the officer had no grounds for asking the defendant to take a test. The police officer may require a test if there is reasonable cause to suspect that any motoring offence has been committed. The police may also stop cars randomly but may only ask for a test if they have reasonable grounds to suspect, having spoken to the driver, that the driver has consumed alcohol.

The defendant may have attempted to blow into the roadside machine but failed to record a reading due to a chest complaint. This would come under the defence available of 'reasonable excuse' for failing to provide a specimen.

If the defendant did give a sample at the roadside, and if that test was positive for alcohol, then the defendant can be arrested although no offence has been proved yet. The proof must come from the police station procedure. The charge may be that the defendant failed to give a specimen in this second procedure rather than the roadside test.

Failing to provide a specimen at the police station is normally contested on the basis that at the police station the defendant blew into the machine but nothing was recorded.

The machines have to take quite a large sample of breath because, at the start of the breath, the reading would be abnormally high due to the residue of alcohol in the defendant's mouth. As the blow progresses, the reading becomes a more accurate reflection of the breath in the lungs. The effect is that you do need to blow reasonably long and hard and sometimes a defendant's attempt does not register at all.

The defendant must do their best to provide a specimen and it is for the defendant to show that they have discharged this duty when the machine failed to take a reading. The officer who observes the procedure will look for evidence of any effort at all being made to blow into the machine.

In any case involving excess alcohol or refusal to give specimens there are procedures that must be followed precisely. These are summary offences so you are not entitled to see the forms on which all the procedure is recorded. The Crown Prosecution Service (CPS) normally discloses them without the need for applying to the court for disclosure. Read them very carefully and make sure that the correct procedure was followed in your client's case.

Punishment
For failing to provide a specimen at the *roadside,* the penalty is a discretionary disqualification, a fine and an obligatory endorsement of four penalty points.

If the failure to provide a specimen was at the police station, and if the defendant was driving or attempting to drive, then the penalty is up to six months' custody, a fine at level 5 with obligatory disqualification and an endorsement of three to 11 penalty points. If the defendant was 'in charge' the maximum penalty falls to three months' custody, fine to level 4, any disqualification is discretionary, but the endorsement of 10 penalty points is compulsory.

Endorsements and 'totting up' (s 35 of the Road Traffic Act 1988)

Most driving offences will require the court to endorse the driver's licence with a minimum number of penalty points. A guide indicating the level of endorsement can be found in Appendix 5.

Ordinarily, a driver is allowed a maximum of 12 points on their licence before they will be disqualified for a six-month period – this is commonly known as 'totting up' although the phrase is borrowed from an earlier system. The period of six months is the recommended period for a person who has not been disqualified for more than 56 days in the last three years. This is called a mandatory sentence, but if the court finds that there are mitigating features it may impose a shorter period than six months – or even no disqualification at all.

For people who have already been disqualified (for over 56 days) in the last three years, then the recommended period of disqualification is one year. It moves up to two years if there have been two disqualifications in the last three years.

What counts as mitigation in terms of discounting the normal effects of totting up is rather limited. It is generally a matter of showing that the disqualification would lead to 'exceptional hardship' (see below).

Where an offender commits more than one endorsable offence at the same time, all of the offences will attract points but the licence will only be endorsed with the number of points attributed to the most serious offence; for example where the defendant has no insurance and a defective light, there will be six points for the insurance matter and three points for the light: the licence will only show six points but two offences.

Where an offender falls to be sentenced and already has a large number of points on their licence and a totting up disqualification looks inevitable, the advocate should ask the court to consider a shorter period of disqualification for the offence on which they await sentence, to avoid totting up. However, where the court declines the submission and disqualifies through totting up, the effect of the disqualification is that the driving licence will be wiped clean at the end of the period of disqualification.

Some offences carry disqualification *and* obligatory endorsement. The effect of this is that the defendant may suffer disqualification, which is imposed for a single offence and not as the result of 'totting up', *and* will have a number of points on the licence on the expiry of the ban making the defendant liable to be disqualified by totting up should they commit any further road traffic offences.

Advocacy in the Magistrates' Court

New drivers

New rules exist for those drivers who commit an offence within two years of passing their test. Whilst their licence can still be endorsed, they are only allowed to accrue a maximum of six penalty points. If their licence is revoked through totting up they will be required to complete a second driving test successfully before qualifying for a full driving licence.

Unlike totting up for the more experienced driver, revocation of a licence does not mean that the slate is wiped clean. Any points imposed leading to the revocation will remain on the licence and will be effective for the normal three-year period from the date of commission of the offence.

Avoiding 'totting up' disqualifications and 'exceptional hardship'

As mentioned above, there are 'mandatory' terms of disqualification that are imposed when a driver reaches 12 penalty points. These 'mandatory' terms can be reduced but in considering whether to do so, the courts are specifically *barred* from considering:

- any facts that are alleged to make the offence less serious;
- hardship other than exceptional hardship;
- any circumstances taken into account on previous occasions when the defendant was before the court on a driving matter.

This does not leave very much, and the reality is that the only ground that is routinely invoked and recognised is 'exceptional hardship'. The advocate must note, however, that it is only open to a defendant to argue exceptional hardship if they have never successfully relied on such an argument in previous proceedings. The court expects a defendant to learn from experience.

Exceptional hardship arguments usually focus upon the effect that a period of disqualification would have on the defendant or their dependants. For example, where the defendant relies upon driving for their job, the court might consider exceptional hardship if a ban would lead to a defendant losing that job. When considering this the court should be furnished with evidence indicating whether other forms of transport are available, whether other people's jobs relied on the defendant's legal entitlement to drive them to work, whether anyone in the defendant's family is under a disability and relies upon the defendant to drive them for treatment, etc.

Where the court finds exceptional hardship it may exercise its discretion and elect not to disqualify for the minimum 'mandatory' period or not to endorse the defendant's licence.

Any advocate seeking to establish exceptional hardship must call the defendant to give sworn evidence about the exceptional hardship that would be faced. If a defendant is later shown to have lied about the consequences of any ban, they could be charged with perjury.

Defence advocates should beware. The word 'exceptional' is interpreted as being a stringent test for any defendant. Almost all driving bans lead to considerable hardship. The defendant's case must be exceptional for the plea to be successful.

Special reasons

'Special reasons' can only be argued in road traffic cases. A special reason is a reason why a defendant should not receive a 'mandatory' disqualification or penalty points even though the offence has actually been proved.

A special reason therefore cannot be a defence. A special reason applies to a driver who is guilty of an offence. A special reason is not a point of personal mitigation for the driver. A special reason relates to the reason why the defendant drove. Someone who drove a car with excess alcohol but only did so to move a car a few metres to allow a fire engine to pass might argue special reasons. The defendant is effectively saying that there was a reason for driving that makes the usual penalty entirely inappropriate.

There is no list of what is or is not a special reason. Four minimum criteria must be fulfilled for any argument to amount to a special reason. The criteria are stated in the case of *R v Wickens* (1958) 42 CAR 236 and are as follows:

- the special reason must be a mitigating or extenuating circumstance;
- it must not amount in law to a defence to the charge;
- it must be directly connected with the commission of the offence; and
- it must be one that the court ought to take into consideration when imposing sentence.

The best source of examples of special reasons can be found in *Wilkinson's Road Traffic Offences* (21st edn, 2003, London: Sweet & Maxwell).

One of the most usual 'special reasons' raised is the shortness of distance driven. Because of its popularity as a special reason there is case law on the matter. Shortness of distance can certainly be argued, but other factors must also be considered for the argument to succeed. In *Chatters v Burke* (1986) 3 AER 168, these matters are as follows:

- how far the vehicle was driven;
- in what manner it was driven;
- the state of the vehicle;
- whether the driver intended to go further;
- the road and traffic conditions prevailing at the time;
- whether there was a possibility of danger by coming into contact with other road users or pedestrians;
- what the reason was for the car being driven.

The onus of proof of establishing special reasons is on the defendant and the standard of proof is on the balance of probabilities. Special reasons must be supported by evidence and not mere assertions by advocates. The defendant would need to be called to give sworn evidence.

Even if a court finds that special reasons exist, the court *may* still disqualify or endorse. The finding of special reasons entitles the court to exercise its discretion if it sees fit. In practice, the court will do so in almost every case.

Procedure for arguing special reasons

Remember that most road traffic cases are put in long lists and are dealt with in a minute or two. If you have not indicated to the court in advance that there will be a special reasons argument, the likelihood is that there will not be time to hear the argument that day.

The procedure would run as follows:

1   The defendant pleads guilty or is convicted of an offence.

2   The Defence will indicate that there will be a special reasons argument.

3   The court will consider how long it will take to argue and will either hear it or adjourn the case to another time.

4   When it comes to the hearing, the defendant gives evidence, and the Defence could call other witnesses to support the evidence of the defendant. It is rare for the Prosecution to call any evidence to rebut the special reason argument.

5   The defence advocate examines the defendant in-chief. They can lead on the fact that the defendant has been convicted of the offence, but then ask what the circumstances of the driving were.

6   The prosecutor may or may not conduct a cross-examination. Prosecutors will often take a fairly neutral stance and leave the matter between the Defence and the sentencing court.

7   Defence advocates have the right to make an address on why the evidence should amount to a special reason and therefore why the court should not impose the normal 'mandatory' sentence.

8   The bench will return a decision on whether a special reason applies to the case. The bench will then go on to sentence, perhaps hearing from the Defence on any other matters of mitigation and the defendant's means.

What if ...?

- *The defendant does not have their licence at court?*

If disqualification is a consideration in a case, the court will need the defendant's licence. If it has been lost, then the court is able to obtain a printout of the licence from the Driver and Vehicle Licensing Authority. Once the court knows about the current state of the licence, it passes the appropriate sentence.

If the defendant lives locally and has attended the court without the licence, the court may grant the defendant some time to return home and collect it. Before releasing your client to do so, you must ensure that the court is in agreement!

If (1) the offence is minor *and* (2) the court is considering a moderate number of points and not disqualification *and* (3) the defendant is not at risk of totting up, then there is another option. This is to put the defendant into the witness box and swear that they have a clean licence (or give evidence of the number of points). The court can then simply award the penalty points. The obvious advantage is that it is not necessary for everyone to come back on another occasion.

If it transpires that the defendant had penalty points and *was* at risk of disqualification, then the defendant runs the risk of a charge of perverting the course of justice! If the defendant is not absolutely sure of what is on the licence do not even suggest this route.

- *The defendant holds a foreign licence?*

Occasionally, the defendant will be the holder of a foreign driving licence. If they are awarded penalty points the DVLC will create an English driving record for them. A foreign driving licence cannot be endorsed.

18   Youth courts

Whilst very similar to the magistrates' court in many respects, the youth court presents a practitioner with additional matters to consider.

Using the right terms

A juvenile is anyone under the age of 18. This sub-divides into 'children' who are under 14 and 'young persons' which covers 14- to 17-year-olds inclusive.

Be careful to identify the 'probation officer', who is not called a probation officer in the youth court but a member of 'the youth justice team'.

Convictions tend to be called 'findings of guilt' and hence a list of previous convictions is likewise referred to as a list of 'findings of guilt'.

The 'appropriate adult'

It is mandatory for a defendant under the age of 16 to be accompanied by a parent or other suitable guardian unless it would be unreasonable to require so in the circumstances. Where the defendant is aged 16 or 17 the court has a discretion to require the attendance of their parent or guardian.

With 16- to 17-year-olds practice really seems to vary on the extent to which a court enquires into the need to have an appropriate adult present.

Once a case is called on, the court clerk/legal adviser will identify the defendant and will then normally ask your help in introducing the appropriate adult to the court.

Give yourself time

Everything takes a little longer in the youth court since the juvenile must be able to follow what is going on. This is equally applicable to your conferences. You may find that the defendant is very unforthcoming and reticent and slow to divulge instructions, and there may be times when everything seems overwhelming to the client and communication becomes really quite hard.

Some juveniles will try to act older and more streetwise than they are, and they will try to show maturity by being quite hostile to proceedings. This can take a while to break down.

Some juveniles will find the presence of their parent or social worker excruciatingly embarrassing and will find it very hard to put the presence of these people out of their mind. It may be that you ask to have a few moments with the client alone without the appropriate adult, but the adult may take exception to this and put you in a difficult position. You simply have to use your judgment.

Conversely, it may be that the defendant does not really know or trust you, and you have to communicate through the appropriate adult who you hope will assure the defendant that you are speaking sense and that you are not some agent for the Prosecution in disguise.

In any event, the message is *get to court early* and give yourself time.

Layout of a youth court

On entering the youth court, the advocate will note that the layout of the court differs considerably from the adult magistrates' court. Proceedings are frequently conducted with parties sitting around a u-shaped table. The three magistrates or District Judge will be seated at one end and clockwise from them will be: the legal adviser, prosecutor, defence advocate, the defendant and their parent, the youth offending team and the witness box.

It is now usual for all parties to remain seated during the hearing but it is advisable to check the system used at your court with the usher. The defendant and witnesses only stand to confirm their name and details and to be sworn in prior to giving evidence. Any witness, whether adult or youth, will take a special youth court oath – there is no bible or separate affirmation. A witness merely promises to 'tell the truth, the whole truth and nothing but the truth'.

Mode of address and language

Once the formalities of identifying the parties are over, advocates must remember that the defendant and all witnesses under the age of 18 should be addressed using their first name only. However, if there is more than one person sharing the same name it is important to ensure that the defendant and any juvenile witness understands how you will differentiate between them. You will also find that juveniles often refer to the other parties involved using nicknames. It is acceptable to adopt such names as long as you confirm their correct name with the juvenile for the benefit of the court at the earliest opportunity.

The practitioner must ensure that any juvenile participating in the hearing easily understands the language being used. In certain cases (such as those involving sexual offences) it may be necessary for juveniles to give evidence on subjects that they find uncomfortable or embarrassing. You may find that they will use nicknames for genitalia and breasts. It is vital that you identify the body part to which they are referring, either by asking them to point to the part in question or otherwise, at the relevant juncture of their evidence. However, once this has been done, allow them to continue to use the language that they are comfortable with.

One must take things a little slower than would be normal in the adult court. Juveniles are often shy and reluctant to speak up in court. Consequently, it is advisable when conducting their evidence to ask simple questions first which will boost their confidence and make them more comfortable with the proceedings. Remember that some juveniles will have difficulty reading and, therefore, you must read out any statement or documents that you are questioning them about. It may be prudent to confirm that a juvenile can read before passing them such a document.

Who can attend?

It is not uncommon for other parties to wish to attend the hearing. However, youth court proceedings are closed to people other than:

- the defendant;
- their parent or guardian;
- legal representatives;
- members and officers of the court;
- the youth offending team officer;
- the press (although subject to stringent reporting restrictions);
- anyone else authorised by the court.

If you are waiting to be called on, it can be particularly difficult to speak to the prosecutor as defence lawyers are not entitled to come into court during other cases. The court accepts this as a systemic problem and will normally be content to rise to vacate the courtroom between cases to let the defence advocate speak to the prosecutor on any matter concerning the case. If you need the court to rise, simply ask the bench when your case is called on.

Mode of trial in the youth court

A juvenile has no right of election. The defendant *will* be tried by the youth court unless the court commits the case.

The case can get to the Crown Court under the two heads listed below.

Grave crimes and s 91 of the Powers of Criminal Courts (Sentencing) Act 2000

The maximum penalty available in the youth court is two years. The youth court cannot exceed this under any circumstances, but the Crown Court can. There are two conditions. First, the conviction must have been in the Crown Court. If the magistrates hear the plea or hold the trial then there is no power to commit to the Crown Court or to exceed the two-year penalty.

The second condition is that the offence must be classified as a 'grave crime'. An offence is categorised as a grave crime if it is an offence which, if committed by an adult, could carry a custodial sentence of 14 years or more (such as aggravated burglary of a dwelling, robbery, grievous bodily harm, etc). For 14- to 17-year-olds only, the list includes the additional offences of indecent assault, causing death by dangerous or careless (whilst being under the influence of drink or drugs) driving.

When dealing with a grave crime before a plea is entered or registered, the court can consider committing to the Crown Court if it feels that its powers are insufficient. The court's powers vary according to the age of the juvenile, so the court must review what its powers are and then decide if the offence *could* warrant more.

The general maximum penalty available to the youth court is two years' detention and training. This is the only consideration for 15- to 18-year-olds. For those who are aged 12 to 14, the court can only order detention if the case is so serious that only a custodial sentence can be justified *and* the defendant is a 'persistent offender'. There is no particular definition of 'persistent offender'. The court can find that a person without previous convictions is still a persistent offender if there are several related offences charged. Therefore, if the court is of the view that a custodial sentence would be justified for a single 'grave' offence where the defendant plainly is not a 'persistent offender', then the court would *have* to commit the defendant to the Crown Court since the youth court would have no power to pass a custodial sentence otherwise.

For those aged 10 or 11, the courts must add the additional requirement that only a custodial sentence would adequately protect the public from that person.

Committal alongside an adult co-defendant

The youth court can commit a juvenile who has a co-defendant who is going to be tried in the Crown Court. There are good reasons for keeping defendants together and good reasons for keeping juveniles in the youth courts. How to resolve the issue depends on how young and potentially vulnerable the defendant is as against the need to have the trial heard in one go. In general terms, the need to keep juveniles in the youth court would seem the more pressing priority.

The adult and juvenile should only have their cases heard together out of the youth court if it is 'in the interests of justice'. The 'interests of justice' test is about fairness and the logic of having both defendants tried together. One should not take account of cost and expedition.

Decisions relating to bail

The youth court, as with all other courts, is bound by the general presumption in favour of bail. However, where a juvenile is charged with a serious offence (as defined in s 25 of the Criminal Justice and Public Order Act 1994) a detention in custody is permissible. By s 23 of the Children and Young Persons Act (CYPA) 1969, if a child or young person under the age of 17 is remanded or committed for trial or sentence and is not bailed, then they must be remanded to local authority accommodation unless the criteria laid down in s 23(5) of the CYPA 1969 are satisfied. If these are satisfied then the court must remand to a remand centre or to prison.

In considering bail the magistrates must take account of the juvenile's own need for protection and welfare. Ordinarily, remand will be into the care of the local authority. It is often important for the defence advocate to liaise with probation, social services and the youth offending team prior to making any representations to the court. Not only will the court need to be satisfied that remand is necessary for the juvenile's protection and welfare, but in times when there are limited places for the remand of juveniles, the court will need to know whether the decision to remand can be put into practice.

When considering whether the criteria in s 23(5) of the CYPA 1969 are satisfied, the court must consider the following:

- the option is only open to a child who has attained 12 years of age;

- the defendant is charged with or has been convicted of a violent or sexual offence, or an offence punishable in the case of an adult with imprisonment for a term exceeding 14 years; *or*

- he or she has a recent history of absconding while remanded to local authority accommodation and is charged with or has been convicted of an imprisonable offence committed during the period of that remand; *and*

- in either case, the court is of the opinion that only a remand to prison or a specific remand centre would be adequate to protect the public from serious harm from the juvenile.

Conditions of bail are just as prevalent and relevant for the youth court as for the adult court. Where the court is considering a surety to secure the juvenile's attendance, then that surety must come from the parent or guardian but is limited to a maximum level of £50. The court may require the parent or guardian to ensure that the juvenile complies with other conditions or forfeit the surety by virtue of s 3(7) of the Bail Act 1976. A requirement under this section can only be imposed with the consent of the parent or guardian.

Other conditions include:

- night time curfew orders;
- reporting to the local police station;
- residence;
- attendance at the offices of the relevant youth justice team to allow reports to be produced;

- restriction of entry into a certain area(s);
- not to contact witnesses directly or indirectly;
- no association with the co-accused.

Many local areas have specialist bail support groups designed to help juvenile offenders who are remanded on conditional bail. It is often a good idea to liaise with the youth offending team which will be able to put the juvenile into contact with these organisations.

Special measures

By its very nature the youth court often finds itself dealing with juvenile witnesses. Recently, special measures directions under the Youth Justice and Criminal Evidence Act (YJCEA) 1999 have come into force. An advocate must always consider whether special measures are needed for their witnesses as applications for special measures must be made at the earliest opportunity. In considering this it is important to know which measures are available at the different court centres.

The special measures that are available include the following:

- screening the witness from the accused;
- giving of evidence by live TV link;
- video recorded evidence-in-chief;
- video recorded cross-examination and re-examination (very rare);
- examination of a witness through an intermediary (very rare).

For a young witness to be eligible for this assistance they must be under the age of 17 at the time of the hearing, or in a situation where the court considers that the quality of their evidence is likely to be diminished by reason of mental disorder, significant impairment of intelligence and social functioning or where they have a physical disability or are suffering from a physical disorder.

Witnesses over the age of 17 are only eligible for special measures in three circumstances:

- Where the offence charged is a sexual offence or one of a violent nature *and* the court has considered any views expressed by that witness and believes the likely diminution in the quality of their evidence would justify the use of special measures.

- Where the prospect of testifying causes the witness fear or distress.

- Where the witness was under the age of 17 at the time of giving video testimony about the offence but has reached the age of 17 at the time of the hearing.

Part II, Chapter I, s 16(3) of the YJCEA 1999 provides that the 'time of the hearing' means the time when it falls to the court to make a determination as to whether special measures should be allowed.

Where special measures have been granted it is important for the advocate whose witness it is to explain fully the procedure to both the witness and their appropriate adult, who must accompany them during their testimony.

Sentencing

First time offenders

Recent changes have been made regarding juvenile sentencing. In particular, where a juvenile comes before the court with no previous convictions and pleads guilty, the court is limited to the following sentencing options:

- an absolute discharge;
- a referral order;
- a detention and training order;
- a hospital order.

These provisions under the Powers of Criminal Courts (Sentencing) Act 2000 exist for offenders aged 10 to 17 years. The most usual order is a referral order; this must be for a minimum of three months and a maximum of nine months, the length of which should reflect the seriousness of the case. The ceiling is set at nine months in all but the most extreme cases and those where the guilty plea is entered at a very late stage. In these situations, they can be extended to run for 10 to 12 months.

It goes without saying that if the offence is so serious that a referral order cannot be considered, the only other valid option will be a period of custody. Before a period of custody is imposed, an advocate should ask the court to have reports prepared regarding the background of the juvenile so as to assist the court in deciding the length of the period of detention.

If a juvenile (who has no previous convictions) has pleaded guilty to one matter but continues to trial on others and is convicted and the sentencing hearing for all offences takes place simultaneously, then the court is once again confined to the limited sentencing options mentioned above. Therefore, it is important when representing a juvenile who intends to plead guilty to some matters but has other matters outstanding that the sentencing process is not rushed, because a subsequent conviction on the other matters may allow a more severe penalty than would have been available had all the matters been sentenced in one instance.

In circumstances where a juvenile does have previous convictions, the court has various sentences available to it dependent upon the seriousness of the crime and the age of the offender. Please see Appendix 3.

Advocacy in the Magistrates' Court

19　Video link courts

What is video link?

Video link is a scheme that is currently being piloted, where the defendant is not brought to court, but rather the advocate and the court communicate with the defendant over a video link system.

There is not a great deal to be said about this, but there are just a few points that it would be helpful to bear in mind.

Which cases are chosen for video link?

Almost any hearing other than trial could be listed as a video link case. It would not be appropriate to conduct any hearing of evidence on a video link, nor are trials listed for hearing by video link, but almost all other proceedings might be listed in this way.

What is the procedure?

You may have been told that your hearing is listed for a video court but do not assume that you will have prior knowledge of this. You may be sent to attend a first appearance and only find on arrival that you have no client at court. Your client remains at the prison, and you will have a slot to speak to the client on a video link.

The timings are critical and by far the most important point about the whole procedure is that you need to be ready when your time is called. In any court that has video link, you do need to be there early and ready in case your slot is an early one. The prison may be linking up to a number of magistrates' courts around the area, and it is not easy to make up lost time.

There will be a room separate from the court where there is a screen and a telephone-style handset. The usher will show you in, and will call the prison for you. When the prison receives the call, the video will appear, and there will be a prison officer ready to get your client for you.

When your client is brought in and the conference is set up, then the usher will leave you in peace for the 10 minutes or so allotted to you. You then have the conference.

When your time is up, the usher will come back in again. You will normally have a time for the hearing of the case (unlike other courts where there is simply a list). You attend court at the appointed time. The courtroom also has a link to the prison and the defendant will watch the proceedings from the prison.

Look out for the view of the court in the top corner of the screen. This shows you what the defendant can see. Make sure that the defendant can see you!

Things to watch out for

There are two problems that seem to have emerged. The first is that once your conference is over, you cannot really speak to your client again in private. When you leave the conference room, there are unlikely to be any more slots available. Once in court, the other link can be used to speak to the defendant, but the defendant's replies are broadcast to the whole courtroom, not just to you. To speak in private you would need to ask everyone to vacate the courtroom!

All that you can do is to be as well prepared as possible and take all instructions that you can and anticipate any question that you can from the bench. If you are making a bail application you had better check every possible condition and its suitability.

The second problem comes when you would otherwise endorse your brief. If you really think that it would be appropriate to endorse the brief before proceeding, then it would seem that you are left with little option other than to ask to adjourn the case to another date and ask on that occasion for the defendant to be produced at court where you can secure an endorsement. If this seems too cumbersome, you will simply have to make a very clear note of what happened and perhaps arrange for an endorsement to be sent to the defendant to sign forthwith.

Asking not to be adjourned to a video court

There may be reasons why the next hearing of the case should not be done in a video court. The obvious one is where the case is more complex and the time allotted simply is not going to be long enough. The court may ask whether it would be feasible for a conference to take place between hearings in the prison. If the adjournment is going to be for only a short time this may be wishful thinking and you would still want to argue that the easiest and cheapest way for the case to progress would be by having the defendant attend court for a long conference on the next occasion.

Similarly, if the case is likely to be very long (eg, you intend to make a long application for bail on the next occasion) it may be better to have the longer hearings in the courts without the video link. This is because of the ever-pressing need not to let cases overrun. One prison may have links to a number of courts and if one court is running past the allotted time, then it can have knock-on effects.

Appendix 1: Typical court layout

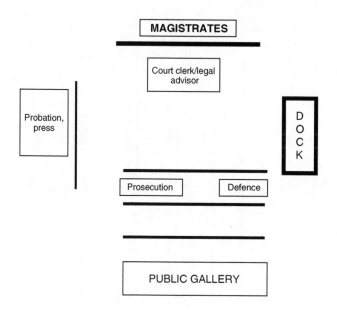

Appendix 2: Plea before venue flowchart

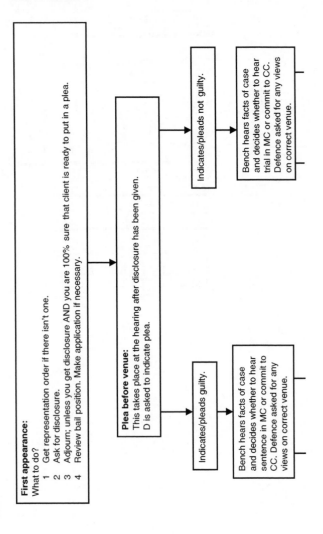

First appearance:
What to do?
1. Get representation order if there isn't one.
2. Ask for disclosure.
3. Adjourn; unless you get disclosure AND you are 100% sure that client is ready to put in a plea.
4. Review bail position. Make application if necessary.

Plea before venue:
This takes place at the hearing after disclosure has been given.
D is asked to indicate plea.

Indicates/pleads guilty.

Bench hears facts of case and decides whether to hear sentence in MC or commit to CC. Defence asked for any views on correct venue.

Indicates/pleads not guilty.

Bench hears facts of case and decides whether to hear trial in MC or commit to CC. Defence asked for any views on correct venue.

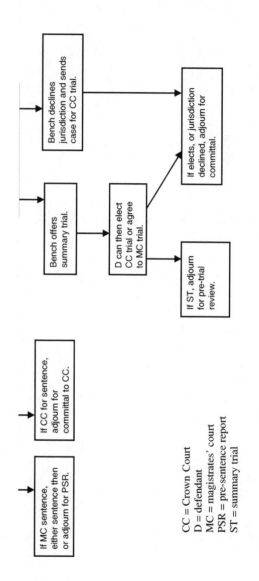

If MC sentence, either sentence then or adjourn for PSR.

If CC for sentence, adjourn for committal to CC.

Bench offers summary trial.

Bench declines jurisdiction and sends case for CC trial.

D can then elect CC trial or agree to MC trial.

If elects, or jurisdiction declined, adjourn for committal.

If ST, adjourn for pre-trial review.

CC = Crown Court
D = defendant
MC = magistrates' court
PSR = pre-sentence report
ST = summary trial

209 **Appendix 2: Plea before venue flowchart**

Appendix 3: Sentence grid

Type of sentence	Must the offence be imprisonable?	Age	Minimum	Maximum	PSR	SSR	Other requirements/ comments
Absolute Discharge	No	10–17	–	–	No	No	Suitable where the court does not want to punish and feels that D is morally blameless.
Referral Order	No	10–17	3 months	12 months	No	No	Refers to first time offenders.
Conditional Discharge	No	10–17	None	3 years	No	No	Cannot be given where D has received a final warning within the previous two years. If D commits a further offence within the period of the discharge then he falls liable to be re-sentenced.
Fine	No	10–13	None	£250	No	No	Financial circumstances of the offender/parent must be taken into account.
		14–17	None	£1000			
Reparation Order	No	10–17	None	24 hrs over 3 months	No	Yes	Allows offender to make amends to the victims of crime.

Type of sentence	Must the offence be imprisonable?	Age	Minimum	Maximum	PSR	SSR	Other requirements/comments
Action Plan Order	No	10–17	3 months	3 months	No	Yes	Can include specified activities.
Attendance Centre Order	Yes	10–13	12 hrs*	12 hrs	No	No	Centre must be reasonably accessible. * Can be reduced if 12 hrs is excessive. $ Can be increased to 24 hrs only if 12 are inadequate.
	Yes	14–15	12 hrs	24 hrs $	No	No	
	Yes	16–17	12 hrs	36 hrs	No	No	
Supervision Order	No	10–17	None	3 years	No	No	Normally the court will ask for a PSR when considering this. Specific requirements can be included in the order.
Community Rehabilitation Order (CRO)	No	16–17	6 months	3 years	No	No	PSR normally ordered but no legal requirement.
Community Punishment Order (CPO)	Yes	16–17	40 hrs	240 hrs	No	Yes	

211 Appendix 3: Sentence grid

Type of sentence	Must the offence be imprisonable?	Age	Minimum	Maximum	PSR	SSR	Other requirements/ comments
Community Punishment and Rehabilitation Order (CPRO)	Yes	16–17	40 hrs 1 year	100 hrs 3 years	No	No	PSR will normally be obtained. This is for the most serious offences which would still fall into the community penalty bracket.
Drug Treatment and Testing Order (DTTO)	No	16–17	6 months	3 years	Yes	No	Consent of D is required for this Order and the Order will be subject to frequent review by the court.
Curfew Order	No	10–17	Up to 3 months if under 16. Otherwise up to 6 months (2–12 hrs per day)		No	No	Consider other people at the address, employment, education and religious beliefs. A PSR will normally be obtained.
Detention and Training Order (DTO)	Yes	12–17	4 months	24 months	Yes	No	DTO will be followed by a period of supervision. If the offender is under 15 years at date of conviction DTO only available if he is a persistent young offender (PYO).

PSR = pre-sentence report; SSR = specific sentence report; D = defendant

Appendix 4: Guide to drugs

Drug	Class	Slang term	How it's taken	Purity and value	Comments
Heroin	A	'H', brown, smack, horse, gear.	Usually diluted in water and injected or inhaled off foil (chasing the dragon).	Cut down to about 10–15%. Sold in small wraps for anything between £5–£15.	Very strong pain killer, and gives a buzz and sense of well-being. Addictive. Often need increasingly large amounts to feel effect.
Cocaine	A	Charlie, coke, white (maybe called blow or whizz if cut with amphetamine).	Generally snorted up the nose, but can be injected in liquid formulation.	Generally cut down to about 30%. Cutting agent could be vitamin C, baking powder, glucose, talcum powder, starch, etc. Value about £40–£60 per gram.	Short hit. Psychologically addictive; user feels very good for short period. Can be problems after with depression and paranoia.

Drug	Class	Slang term	How it's taken	Purity and value	Comments
Crack Cocaine	A	Base, stones, rocks.	Crack is the smokable form of cocaine. The cocaine is made into small 'rocks' with baking soda and water. It makes a cracking noise when smoked. This could be through a pipe, tube, bottle or foil. The effects are much stronger than powdered cocaine, with each subsequent hit taking the user higher (this is not the case with powdered cocaine).	Variable purity and value. Huge regional variations due to supply and availability of drug. A small rock (size of a peanut) could cost £10–£20.	Very strong short lived hit. Highly addictive, physically and mentally. User feels exhilarated, etc, but can feel very bad after high.
LSD	A	Acid, cheer, smiles, often referred to by the artwork on the paper (rainbow, strawberry).	Sold as squares of 'paper' or as pellet or liquid. Taken orally.	Variable value and purity of the active component. Normally £1–5 for a tab.	LSD is hallucinogenic. It is not addictive. Can take a while to take effect, and so some users think it's not working and take more.

Drug	Class	Slang term	How it's taken	Purity and value	Comments
PMA	A	Mitsubishi, killer, chicken fever, double stacked.	In pills like ecstasy only bigger.	£3–8. New drug, not much research on purity levels.	This drug is much like ecstasy but much stronger; up to 20 times stronger in fact.
MDMA (Ecstasy)	A	E, pills, disco biscuits, tabs, or a name referring to the artwork on the pill itself.	Swallowed as a pill or as liquid capsule.	£3–8 according to the amounts available in the area. Used to be £10–15 in the '90s.	Clubbers' drug. Gives energy and makes people feel loving. Can make you dehydrate and overheat quickly.
Methadone	A	Morphine, methadone, opium.	Prescription methadone is usually a syrup. Other derivatives of methadone come as fluid to inject.	Usually prescription drugs that have found their way onto the street. Value about £1 per 10ml.	Does not have the buzz of heroin, but removes pain and anxiety and induces feeling of well-being and tranquility. Used in reducing prescriptions to break addiction to heroin.
Amphetamines (Speed)	B	Billy, whizz, base amphetamine.	Normally sold as a powder in a wrap and taken by rubbing on gums, snorting or swallowing.	Heavily cut drug, purity about 5–10% generally. Sold at about £10 a wrap.	This is a clubbers' drug that gives energy to the taker. Can inspire paranoia, depression, etc, after the 'high'. Can lead to short term memory loss.

215 Appendix 4: Guide to drugs

Drug	Class	Slang term	How it's taken	Purity and value	Comments
Cannabis	B (plans to re-classify to C)	Hundreds of names. Commonly called: blow, hash, grass, skunk, pot, weed, backy, etc.	Cannabis *resin* is the resin from the plant, which comes in a brown sticky block. Otherwise, users take the leaves or flowers and dry them. Usually, cannabis is mixed with tobacco and smoked, but it can be infused in tea or put in cakes.	Cannabis is not generally diluted with anything. The active ingredient of cannabis is called THC. The THC levels are much higher in the flowering head than in the leaves. Some strains of cannabis are more potent. 'Skunk' is a potent form of cannabis, but the word is now commonly used as to describe any good quality cannabis and flowering heads. Cannabis is usually sold in fractions of ounces. The smallest cut is a 16th of an ounce (called a 'teenth'). Other measures are an eighth (called a 'Henry'), a quarter, etc. A teenth is about £7.	Cannabis is often 'home grown'. The plants need lots of light. The plants are either grown in earth or in water trays (called hydroponics). A sophisticated growing system will have water trays, CO_2 gas canisters, lighting on-timer switches, strong fluorescent lighting and hydroponic trays.

Appendix 5: Road traffic penalties

Offence	Code	Penalty	Licence/points
Accident, failing to give particulars	AC20	Level 5 fine and/or 6 months	E 5–10
Accident, fail to report	AC20	Level 5 fine and/or 6 months	E 5–10
Accident, fail to stop	AC10	Level 5 fine and/or 6 months	E 5–10
Brakes, defective (private vehicle)	CU10	Can be dealt with as fixed penalty or level 4 fine	E*3 (only endorse if driver should have known of defect)
Breath test, refusing	DR70	Level 3 fine	E 3–11
Careless driving	CD10	Level 4 fine	E 3–9
Dangerous condition, using a private vehicle in ...	CU20	Can be dealt with as fixed penalty or level 4 fine	E*3 (only endorse if driver should have known of defect)
Defective tyre, private vehicle	CU30	Can be dealt with as fixed penalty or level 4 fine	E*3 (only endorse if driver should have known of defect)
Driving carelessly	CD10	Level 4 fine	E 3–9

Offence	Code	Penalty	Licence/points
Driving dangerously	DD40 (triable either way)	Level 5 fine and/or 6 months	D 3–11
Driving whilst disqualified	BA10	Level 5 fine and/or 6 months	E 6
Driving whilst under influence of drink	DR20	Level 5 fine and/or 6 months	D 3–11
Driving with excess alcohol	DR10	Level 5 fine and/or 6 months	D 3–11
Drunk in charge	DR50	Level 4 fine and/or 3 months	E 10
Failing to produce licence		Level 3 fine	
Failing to produce insurance		Level 3 fine	
Failing to produce MOT		Level 3 fine	
Insurance, using, permitting or causing to drive without	IN10	Level 5 fine	E 6–8
Licence, driving otherwise than in accordance with ... (DOWTIAWL)	LC10	Level 3 fine	E 3–6
Motor Cyclist not wearing helmet		Level 2 fine	
Obstruction, causing unnecessary ...		Level 3 fine	

Offence	Code	Penalty	Licence/points
Pedestrian crossing, failure to give precedence	PC20	Level 3 fine	E 3
Refusing, blood/urine/breath sample (in charge)	DR60	Level 4 fine and/or 3 months	E 10
Refusing, blood/urine/breath sample (driving)	DR30	Level 5 fine and/or 6 months	D 3–11
Speeding, road	SP30	Level 3 fine	E 3–6
Speeding, motorway	SP50	Level 4 fine	E 3–6
Tyre, defective (private vehicle)	CU30	Level 4 fine	E*3 (only endorse if driver should have known of defect)

Please note that this is not a full list of offences and penalties. I have tried to provide you with the most common offences in the Road Traffic Court.

E = the offence attracts obligatory points; the court also has powers of discretionary disqualification.

D = the offence attracts an obligatory disqualification (check whether special reasons apply).

219 Appendix 5: Road traffic penalties

Index